Dyker
Lad

Recollections of Life in an East Neuk of Fife Fishing Village; before, during, and after the Second World War.

Alexander Swanston Davidson Corstorphine

Published by:

Wast-By Books
26 Friday Walk
Lower Largo
Fife
Scotland
KY8 6FB

Edited and Published by James K. Corstorphine

Front Cover: Sonny Corstorphine at the helm of the 'Dyker Lad' in Anstruther's InnerHarbour

Extract From "Tae Jeems"

Written in the 'auld Scots' tongue' by the celebrated Fife bard 'Poetry Peter' Smith, the following lines lamenting the passing of well-known Cellardyke townsfolk has been extracted from one of his best known works:

Wi' sea and land we're sundered far,
An' mony a Dyker's cross't the Bar,
And mony a weel kent lass or chiel,
And mony a ane we lo'ed sae weel,
Hae come, as we say, tae their end.

Yet Jamie, I hae ne'er forgot,
Tae tell ye what we're a' aboot.
Then jist a word aboot the lave,
Baubie's awa, ye ken - and Dave;
And Jeems we really miss them sair,
You ken, what means the vacant chair.

But Jeems, we're no tae sit and greet,
We'll meet them in the Golden Street;
And tho' doon here we miss their faces,
Ithers grow up tae tak' their places;
God willed it so in his great plan,
Oor bit while here is - play the man.

Foreword

My father, Alexander "Sonny" Corstorphine, lived his entire life in the East Neuk fishing village of Cellardyke, on the northern shores of the Firth of Forth.

My Dad led an incredibly interesting life, and it was in 1987 that he first conjured up the idea of writing his memoirs, which has, albeit indirectly, led to the publication of this book.

Initially, his plan was simply to describe his life as a youngster, and illustrate how different life was for children back in the 1930's. However, memories of other events which occurred later in his life kept coming to mind, which he thought were also worthy of recording. For this reason, his memoirs took over twenty years to write, being finally completed in 2007.

After having read his finalised memoirs with great interest, I suggested to Dad that they would make a very interesting book, which would be of interest not only to his family, but to anyone interested in how life was lived before and during World War Two and in the decade or so that followed the conflict.

He gave the matter some thought, but decided that he would rather such a book was not published during his lifetime. He added, however, that "efter ah'm awa', ye can dae as ye like"!

My father passed away in December 2014.

Early in 2018, I discussed with my brothers, David, Neil and Calum, the possibility of publishing these memoirs, and we concurred that the time was now right to compile the story of our father's early life in the form of this book.

James Corstorphine, May 2018.

Contents

A young Sonny Corstorphine pictured with Grandfather David Corstorphine around 1934

Introduction

I was born on the 18th day of April in the year 1931, at 'St. Abbs', West Forth Street, Cellardyke, Fife. My mother was Margaret Corstorphine, a machinist in an oilskin factory.

She was 25 years old when I was born, and was unmarried. I never knew my father, and only found out who he was when I was 58 years old. It seems that a holiday romance didn't work out, and a marriage never took place.

My grandmother chose my names, and I was named as Alexander Swanston Davidson Corstorphine. Firstly, my granny wished me to be named in memory of my uncle, Alexander Swanston Corstorphine, who had lost his life during the Great War of 1914-18; and secondly, in memory of my Aunt Lizzie's husband, Alexander Davidson, who was much respected, and who had died in 1930.

However, it was also decided that I should not be directly called Alex or Alexander, but that instead I would be referred to as 'Sonny', in the tradition of my grandmother's family, the Swanstons of Eyemouth, whenever there had been a duplication of names.

Around the time that I was born, my grandmother, Jane Swanston, was becoming very infirm and crippled, due to severe arthritis in her hands. Therefore, my grandfather gave up his life on the sea, in order to look after her. My Aunt Lizzie, recently widowed, was also asked to look after the family home.

I was brought up to refer to my Aunt Lizzie as "Mum", and I looked on her as being my Mum, not knowing anything else as being the truth, until I was about 12 years old. She was a good Mum to me. I regarded my natural mother as my Auntie Maggie, a role that she played correctly, never giving me any cause to think differently.

However, after I had grown up, and only then discovering the true facts, I realised that Maggie had always played a large part behind the scenes in my upbringing, with her doing any knitting, clothes repairs and other chores, and always being quick to take my side in any of my discords.

I now know how much she must have missed out in her life because of me. I hope that I gave her something back in return in her later years, especially as she was correctly known and referred to, by my children, as being their grandmother.

I have often wished that I had kept a written record of conversations between myself and older members of my family, and in particular, those conversations which I had with my grandfather, David Corstorphine, who was a retired skipper and owner of a steam herring drifter. I had a great respect for my grandfather, and I spent much of my early life in his company.

The conversations I had with my grandfather were always interesting, particularly if any subject of days gone by was mentioned, and were an insight into an earlier way of life that could not return.

I have written these memoirs for a number of reasons, but most importantly I am trying to ensure that my children, my grandchildren, and future generations of my family will have a record of this part of their family history.

Chapter One

Earliest Memories

The earliest memory that I have, when I could only have been about two-and-a-half years old, was of being awakened at about five or six o'clock on a cold morning in early December, amidst a buzz of excitement in our living room, where I slept in a box-bed with my Aunt Lizzie.

The reason for the commotion was because my Uncle Tom had arrived home, at that early hour, from the East Anglian Herring Fishery. The herring drifter on which he was a member of the crew had managed to get into AnstrutherHarbour on the night tide, after completing its journey home from Great Yarmouth.

I had been told that 'Tam' would be bringing me a present from Yarmouth and, on hearing his voice, I wanted to know what my present was, and was therefore immediately wide awake. My present was a small toy aeroplane, which hung from a piece of string, and by winding up a strong elastic band, a propeller then made it go round and round. To the children of fishing families, the Yarmouth present was the big event of the year, and for some reason the Christmas presents which arrived some weeks later did not impart the same excitement.

In later years, I was lucky enough to be the recipient of several such gifts when the fishing fleet returned from the south, including a clockwork train set, and various 'Meccano' sets.

The departure, in early October each year, of the herring drifters to Great Yarmouth for the East Anglian Herring Fishery, was quite a spectacular occasion. Because of their deep draught, the drifters had to wait for high water before they could leave Anstruther harbour, and several vessels would leave on the same tide. The families and friends of the fishermen, together with many onlookers, would gather on the piers beside the boats, to bid their farewells, and to wish them good luck.

It was traditional for the fishermen to hand out a quantity of hardtack boat's biscuits to those people waiting on the pier. In return, after the boats had cast off and were moving through the 'cut' between the inner and outer harbours, and also when going out through the outer harbour mouth, well-wishers would throw coins on to the decks of the drifters, as a symbol of financial good luck.

Many of these coins either missed the boats, or bounced back into the water. Later in the day, at low water, young boys would return to the harbour to search for the coins that had missed the target.

As soon as each drifter cleared the harbour mouth, it would sound its own steam horn or whistle, to let the whole town know that it was on its way.

On the return of the drifters in late November or early December, and after the "pairtin" (parting), where the profits from the fishing were shared out, the skippers would ask the local bakers to produce large shortbread cakes, decorated with a picture of their drifter, drawn in white icing, and showing the boat's name and number. These were usually displayed in the baker's windows for a few days, before being collected and handed out to the members and families of the various crews.

The expected visit from Santa Claus at Christmas did still give me quite a lot of excitement, though, and for a few evenings before the due event the rest of the family were entertained by having me 'cryin' up the lum', to tell Santa what I wanted from him.

The crew of the steam drifter "Unity", KY162. My grandfather, the owner and skipper, is standing on the extreme left. My Uncle Willie is crouched directly in front of him.

Once, when I was about three or four years old, I had been 'cryin' up the lum' to Santa, when the assembled family members told me that they didn't think Santa would be able to hear what I wanted for Christmas as I wasn't shouting loud enough. My Aunt Lizzie, in an attempt to get me to shout louder, instructed me to "cry awfy lood" (shout really loud) up the chimney. So, I again turned my face towards the fireplace, and at the top of my voice shouted the words "awfy lood".

Hanging up a stocking was the usual ritual on Christmas Eve, and I always felt that I must be luckier than most other children, as I was allowed to hang up one of my grandfather's huge sea-boot stockings. Always being wide awake early on Christmas Day, I would retrieve the stocking from the fireplace and take it back into the cosy warm bed to extract its contents. Most of the presents consisted of new items of clothing, such as socks, shirts, pyjamas or some underwear. There would usually be some other small presents, such as books, and often a new pencil case, complete with pencils and a rubber. It was, however, still exciting for me to put my hand deep into the stocking, and find some sweets, an orange and an apple, and lastly a half-crown coin (twelve and a half pence value in today's money).

Uncle Tam, at that time, was always teasing me, and he enjoyed having some fun at my expense. When it was windy, on cold winter nights, a draught could be heard whistling through the passage outside the living room door. After dark, Tam would take the opportunity to tell me the story about a little girl called Lucy Gray, who had got lost, and had been taken away by the wind. He would then ask me to listen to the wind whistling through the passage, before telling me that what we could hear was Lucy Gray, crying and wanting her Mum. This sad story was enough for me to start crying also, which gave him great amusement.

In my pre-school childhood, I also remember going for walks with my grandfather, whom I always called 'Dey', which is what grandfathers were called all along the FifeCoast. These walks were mainly to the harbour at Anstruther, which we commonly referred to as 'Enster'.

The old fishermen always referred to a point of the compass, whenever they were walking anywhere, so from our house, we did not just 'go to Anstruther', but instead, we walked 'Wast tae Enster' (West to Anstruther), and when returning home from there, we 'cam Aist tae Cellardyke' (came East to Cellardyke).

On a fine day, my Dey would take me round the piers at Anstruther, and a favourite walk was to go down the East Pier and climb the iron ladder on to its high wall, then walk back along the top of the wall to its shore end.

Around the harbour, we would stop frequently to have a look at any of the boats moored there, and we would observe the crews occupied in various tasks, for example changing their

A busy scene at AnstrutherHarbour in the 1930's

fishing gear from nets to lines or vice-versa, if the boat was in the process of changing its mode of fishing.

There was always something of interest to be seen around the harbour, and there were always a few retired fishermen to meet up with at the 'weigh hoose' at the top of the West Pier. Here, the news of the day was exchanged, and meantime I was kept quiet with a 'penny mixture', which comprised a small paper bag containing about ten sweets, all taken from various bottles, and all for the sum of one penny (in old pre-decimal money). This bag was usually bought at Kate Finlay's wee greengrocer and sweetie shop, next to the Ship Tavern at the east end of Anstruther's Shore Street.

If rain came on, or if it was a bit too cold to be outdoors, then we would find shelter in Cunningham's net loft, where we would watch the fishermen busily repairing their nets. Cunningham's net loft is now part of the ScottishFisheriesMuseum.

Often, on the way home from 'Enster', we pretended that Dey was the 'big ship', and I was the 'wee tug boat', and I would then pretend to tow him and help him up the brae at the Caddie's Burn. Sometimes, we would drop into Boyter's sail loft, at the west end of West Forth Street, and watch Wullie Boyter and his son Andrew, both busy with palm and needle, making new sails, or repairing old ones, for the drifters in the harbour.

As a youngster, I was given a present of a small pedal go-car, by our neighbours Mr and Mrs Gourlay, after their son Jim had outgrown his toy car, and I spent many happy days pedalling along the pavement in front of our house. I also played a lot in the rear garden of our house, 'St. Abbs', which was completely walled in from the road, and so it was a perfectly safe place for a toddler to play. If the gear-loft was free from any other activity, I was allowed to play there on cold or wet days, where I had a wooden swing, which hung from the beams in the loft.

In the early 1930s, the street lighting in Cellardyke was provided by gas lamps. At that time, these gas lamps did not have automatic time clocks for switching the gas on and off, therefore a lamp-lighter was employed to go round the Cellardyke streets every evening, and light these lamps manually. I must have only been about four years old when my grandfather noted my interest in following and watching the lamp-lighter doing his job, whenever he was in our street. Because of this, my Dey made me a small wooden ladder, about the same length as my own height, which had about four rungs on it. So, when the lamp-lighter (I believe that his name was Willie Pratt) came round to our street at night, I would be waiting for him, and would then accompany him around a few of the lamps, he with his ladder and me with mine, and I pretended to be helping him do his job.

I believe that I was a fairly well-behaved youngster, but I once used the words, "Shut up", and I got such a row that I thought that the world had come to an end. Like many other boys of my time, I lived in fear of the threat of the drastic punishment that would surely come to pass, if I ever strayed from the straight and narrow path of good behaviour.

For telling lies, we believed that "The man o' the moon will lower his cleek an' tak ye awa' ". Another possible punishment was to be 'Sent to the training ship', where we would be subjected to severe discipline and corrective training, but nobody ever told us laddies that the Mars Training ship, which had been anchored in the Tay, near Wormit, for many years, had ceased to function in 1929, two years before I was even born.

However, I think that the most feared punishment of all was that, if I was ever guilty of a wrong-doing, then a 'Black Mark' would be entered in 'God's Book', and when a certain number of these black marks were reached, "Ye'll gan tae the burnin' fire". I believed that this 'burnin' fire' was at the local gas works in East Green. Often, when I was walking past there, and glancing through the big open doors, I would see the coke-ovens being stoked, with big flames belching out. I immediately thought, "That must be because another bad boy is being got rid of", and so I would hurry along the road.

The local hairdresser, John Harrow (known locally as Johnnie Harrie), had his shop in Shore Street, Anstruther. Shore Street was noted for being a sun-trap, as it was always that little bit more sheltered from the wind and thereby often warmer than the other streets. A local saying was that, "The sun is aye shinin' at Johnnie Harrie's door".

Johnnie Harrie had a lathe at home, on which he made various wooden objects, as a hobby. He was a good friend of my grandfather and, one day, he presented me with a 'peerie', a small wooden spinning top, driven with a string whip.

The garret, which was situated on the third floor of our house, was the place where nets were stored and mended, and was therefore at times a busy work-place where my grandfather and my uncles would sit carrying out their various tasks. All of them were smokers, and although my grandfather liked his pipe, all of the others smoked cigarettes. Great amusement was caused when one of my uncles would offer me a puff on his cigarette, and this caused me to back away coughing and spluttering. In my mind, I soon began to protest at them having their fun at my expense, and vowed that I would never allow a cigarette to enter my mouth ever again. That is probably the reason that I never became a smoker.

Chapter Two

The Toon and its Characters

The conjoined township of Cellardyke and Anstruther, in the mid-1930s, was a busy and thriving community. It had survived the depression of the early 1920s, from which it had recovered gradually.

Because Cellardyke had lost out to Anstruther a century earlier in the development of its own harbour, the village consequently could not accommodate a fleet of locally owned fishing boats. The result of this scenario was that the main occupation of the male population of Cellardyke was to provide skippers and crews for the large steam drifters, and other boats, which were based in Anstruther.

New fishing boats were built as the local community emerged from the depression, and the local herring fishing entered a period of prosperity, which was to last until the outbreak of World War II.

The result of this fishing boom was to have its spin-off amongst other businesses in the town, both in the work given to the ancillary trades, and with the reduction in unemployment meaning that extra money was now available to spend in the local shops.

Boatyards, Ship Chandlers, Marine Engineers, Oilskin Manufacturers, Oil and Coal Suppliers and Carters were all to enjoy a direct share in the prosperity, and the town now had a busy bustling atmosphere.

There were now three fish curing businesses in Cellardyke; namely Alex. Scott in Caddie's Burn; Melville's in John Street and Cormack's at the East End.

Also playing their important part in the fishing industry in Cellardyke were three oilskin factories; Robert Watson and Co. in George Street; W. and A. Myles in James Street and John Martin and Co. in East Forth Street; the latter also having a large knitwear manufacturing department.

Sail Makers, Marine Engineers and Joiners were other thriving local businesses that benefiting directly from the fishing boom during the 1930s.

The local population, of course, had to be fed, and there were no fewer than six bakeries in Cellardyke at that time. Most of these businesses had large bake-houses, but one baker operated his business from a local authority house in Toll Road.

There were nine grocers with retail premises in the town, and two greengrocers, who both operated their businesses from horse-drawn carts.

As one would expect in a fishing community, fish and chip shops were popular, and Cellardyke boasted two, both of which were in James Street, and could be easily accessed from our house in West Forth Street by going down the 'Wee Wynd'; a steep pedestrian passageway that connected the two streets, the top of which was just across the street from our house.

The fish and chip shop that was located at the bottom of the Wee Wynd, at its junction with James Street, was operated by Tam Boyter and his wife, Maggie Jane. It opened at 7 pm., and was a regular meeting point for children who had been given a penny for chips. With our penny worth of chips in a brown bag, we would sit in one of his four cubicles, and pour huge quantities of sauce, vinegar, salt and pepper on to them. When Tam, Maggie Jane, or their assistant Belle Gen weren't looking, we would sneak a drink out of the bottles of vinegar. The Boyters could not have made much profit out of us!

*The bottom of the 'Wee Wynd' and the former fish and chip shop
operated by Tam Boyter and his wife, Maggie Jane.*

Tam Boyter was always interested to hear what the herring boats were catching, especially when they were down at Yarmouth, and when the 'word' (news) regarding the individual catches was received from down south and mentioned in the chip shop, he would write the boat's name, and the number of crans caught, on a slate hanging on a wall. News of outstanding catches soon spread through the town thanks to Tam's slate.

There were two dairies in the town; Tom Blyth in West Forth Street, and Thomas Hodge in George Street. Tom Blyth's ten or so cows were pastured in a large field, which was bounded by Fowler Place, Toll Road and Crail Road. The cows had to be brought down to their byre in West Forth Street, by way of Burnside Terrace, around tea-time every day, for milking. The cows were again milked the following morning before being taken back to their field.

Tom Blyth sold his fresh milk, both in the morning and in the evening, from a small room in his house in West Forth Street, and children living and playing nearby would ask Tom if they could go into the byre to see the cows being milked, which was all done by hand into a pail. When I was there on one occasion, Tom asked a few of us to step much closer to see what was happening, and he suddenly turned the teat of the cow which he was milking towards us, and our faces were squirted with a jet of warm milk!

Cellardyke also boasted an ice-cream maker by the name of David Tawse, whose premises were in James Street. He also traded from a barrow which he pushed around the streets in the summer-time. He was always referred to as 'Tawsie', and he was a small fat man with a large round cheery face who liked a bit of fun, especially with children. He always found it a bit of a struggle to push his barrow up the braes, and was very glad when children offered to give him a hand.

He would reward his helpers with a halfpenny cone, which was quite a substantial reward in those days.

Tawsie came up the Wee Wynd, opposite our house, every evening to buy a pitcher of fresh milk from Blyth's dairy, and it was customary for any children, who happened to be around, to ask him to demonstrate how he could turn his pitcher upside down without letting any milk fall out. Being still too young to understand the science of centrifugal force, we were mesmerised by this feat. Tawsie would start off with a few swings backwards and forwards, and then carry on with a full overhead swing, and not spill a drop. One evening, though, the handle came off, and the pitcher went flying down the Wee Wynd, with the contents being splashed all over the ground. We did not dare to laugh!

There were several other thriving businesses in Cellardyke during the 1930s, including four drapers, two butchers, and two shoemakers. Butters, the grocer, also sold shoes.

There was also a sub Post Office in John Street and a branch of the National Bank, which operated from premises in the lower part of the Town Hall.

In contrast to the Cellardyke of more than a century earlier, there was only one public house, that being the Boat Tavern in John Street.

In addition to the above Cellardyke based traders, there were also many mobile traders from Anstruther and other villages, who were to be found in the streets of Cellardyke selling from their carts.

The activities of all of these traders, along with domestic coal delivery, collection of refuse, and a seemingly endless stream of collection and delivery of fishing gear between the boats and the fishermen's houses, meant that there were a lot of carts and also quite a few lorries to be found in the streets of 1930's Cellardyke.

The carts greatly outnumbered the motor vehicles at this time, and they were nearly all horse-drawn. Most of the streets were surfaced with bluestone 'causey setts' and, because most of the carts had metal rims on their wheels, the sound which could be heard when a cart was coming along the road was of the metallic ringing and crunch of these wheels on the streets combined with the clip-clop of the horses' hooves, which were also metal shod.

I remember a number of occasions when a cart had been overloaded, and this caused the horse to slip and fall as it tried to pull the cart up the steep hill at Caddie's Burn. Sometimes, a horse would get its legs entangled in the harness as it fell, and it often took quite a while to disentangle the struggling horse from the ropes and straps and chains. On a few occasions, the horses were hurt badly in these accidents.

Every day, somewhere on the streets, the horses would leave their droppings, and any nearby housewife, if she had a garden, would immediately fetch a pail and shovel to gather up the droppings for use as a fertiliser for roses. Many a time, two housewives would set out for the same pile, and an argument would ensue as to who had most right to the dung!

Looking on, as a young boy, these were exciting times in Cellardyke.

Chapter Three

Our House

Before proceeding further, I would like to describe the house in which I was born and brought up, and the home environment in which I spent my childhood.

'St. Abbs', West Forth Street, Cellardyke, is a three storied house, constructed of stone and built around 1903. It is typical of fishermen's houses of that period, with the front of the house abutting the public pavement, there being no front garden or yard. It was one of two houses erected in a gap site, between numbers 14 and 16 West Forth Street, opposite a terrace of three similar dwellings called the 'Boatie Rows'.

The front door opened into a long passage, which extended right through to the back door. The first few feet of this passage was laid in decorative ceramic tiles, but the rest was laid in plain cement and covered with linoleum. The lower part of the passage walls were panelled in a dark-stained plain wood, which was then heavily varnished; and the upper walls were painted with a light green oil paint. This type of décor had a hygienic purpose, as the surfaces could be easily wiped and cleaned.

The first door on the right of this passage was the door to the kitchen, which also served as the sitting-room and living-room. This room was quite compact, with a coal-fired kitchen range built into the wall opposite the door, surrounded by a wooden mantelpiece, on which was mounted a bracket with a gas lamp. This lamp served as our only source of light on dark nights until the arrival of electricity to the house in the mid-1930s.

In the near left corner of the room, as seen from the door, was a small dark scullery, measuring about five feet by four feet, with a sink in which vegetable preparation and dish-washing was carried out. An enamel basin, placed into this sink, served for personal washing; there being no bathroom in the house during my childhood years.

In the far left corner of the room was a box bed, and this is where I slept with my Aunt Lizzie, until I was about eleven years old.

This bed was completely walled in on three sides, and curtains were hung across its opening. It was very cosy in there and, in my younger days, going to bed early presented no problem, as I could lie in bed and hear all of the conversations taking place in the room, which I particularly enjoyed when we had friends visiting! That was in the days before radio or television, and much of the conversation was centred around experiences and stories about people in days gone by.

Adjacent to the front window, on the south wall, was an eight-day pendulum wall clock. It had a spring drive, which had to be wound up weekly, and its gong struck on every hour and half-hour. It was always kept about ten minutes fast, a peculiarity that I could never fully understand. It has to be said, however, that most homes in Cellardyke had their clocks set around ten minutes ahead of the correct time. In fact, some houses even considered it to be normal to have their clock set half-an-hour fast!

There was only one wooden lightly padded armchair in the room, placed between the bed and the fire, and this was where my grandmother sat. The other chairs in the room were all made of plain wood, without any padding.

Above the fireplace was a large portrait photograph of my late uncle, Alex. Davidson, dressed in naval uniform; and on another wall was a large photograph the Royal Navy football team that he had played for.

A short passageway led off from the rear of the kitchen into the back bedroom, which had its own fireplace and a box bed in which my grandparents slept.

A spiralling anti-clockwise stairway, situated at the far end of the aforementioned long passageway which led from the front to the rear of the house, led to the upper floors.

The rooms on the first floor consisted of two rooms and a scullery; which, in effect, made the first floor a self-contained flat. The reason for this arrangement was so that a family could be accommodated there and live independently from the rest of the house. This lay-out was quite common in the houses of fishing families, and allowed family members to get married and raise families of their own whilst still living within the confines of their family home.

In the front bedroom on the first-floor, where my mother and Aunt Phemie slept, there was a pedal organ; a beautiful piece of furniture, with mirrors built into its upper part, and with a small shelf on either side. On one of these shelves was a photograph of my uncle, Alexander Corstorphine, in Navy uniform. On the other shelf was a grey gunmetal cross-shaped plaque, about six inches square, with a large bronze medallion in its centre. This had an engraving, showing the figure of Britannia, with a lion standing by her side, and an inscription, 'Alexander Swanston Corstorphine'. Around the edge of the medallion was engraved, 'He Died for Freedom and his Country'.

My Uncle Tom, who was a fisherman, slept in the back bedroom on a free standing bed, above which hung a large photograph of my great grandmother, Elisabeth Dougal. I had another two fishermen uncles, Uncle Willie and Uncle David, who had both left the family home before I was born.

Before electricity came to our house, there was no light in the stair; so, when going upstairs to bed during the winter months, a candle in a holder had to be lit for this purpose.

There were gas-lights in all of the bedrooms, and these would be lit whilst undressing and getting ready for bed. Sometimes a small paraffin lamp was lit, and left on the stair window-sill for an hour or two in the evening.

On the top floor of the house, as mentioned in an earlier chapter, was the garret, which had a bare wooden floor with white-washed walls. Originally, the garret occupied the whole of the top floor, but my Uncle George, who was a joiner, built an attic bedroom up there of varnished wood, which utilised the rear garret window. In this room was an open bed, and this was where he slept until he got married in 1940.

The rest of the garret was bare to the rafters, which were always referred to as the 'couples'. The view from the front garret window was somewhat restricted by the terrace of houses on the opposite side of the street. Looking to the right, however, there was a good view of AnstrutherHarbour and the Billowness.

To the left, CellardykeTown Hall and its clock were seen, and this was the clock which my grandfather used for his 'Standard Time'. On returning from a visit to the garret, he would announce the 'correct' time. Not for him, were the new-fangled Greenwich Mean Time pips on the 'wireless', at the start of the news bulletins broadcast at one o'clock and six o'clock!

The main purpose of the garret was to store fishing nets, and it was also a place where these could be repaired. A large beam, with a pulley wheel on the end, could be slid out of the top of the open front garret window, and this was the means by which the nets were hoisted up from street level, after they had been delivered to the front of the house by horse and cart.

The garret was sparsely furnished, with only some bare wooden chairs or stools, and some trestles on which the nets were stowed. There was a metal stove, which was used to heat the garret whenever net-mending was taking place during the winter; usually when the boats could not go to sea because of bad weather.

Always present in the garret was a strong but pleasant smell of cotton, hemp, tarry twine and Hessian bags. The purpose of the latter was for holding the nets and corks. This was where my grandfather, with his sons and cronies, would meet and have a fine blether whenever the nets were being mended.

During a few weeks in the summer months, as a means of supplementing the financial income to the house, the middle flat was let out to summer visitors. These holidaymakers invariably came from Edinburgh, Glasgow and Paisley during their respective Trades Holiday fortnights. This meant that our own sleeping arrangements had to be altered, and therefore the garret became utilised as a spare bedroom for family members. The garret beds consisted of shake-downs placed on the floor, and I always found that sleeping in this situation was an exciting and novel experience.

The old family gramophone had been relegated to the garret and, on rainy days, I would often entertain myself by going up there to play old records. This primitive apparatus, of course, was of the variety that had to have its driving mechanism wound up manually before the records could be played.

Electricity finally arrived in West Forth Street in 1936, and our house was one of the first to be connected. At that time, however, electrical appliances were few and far between, and it was only considered necessary to have a single electric light bulb fitting in each ceiling, and a single five-amp socket in each room. To mark the occasion of electricity arriving in the locality, the Fife Electric Power Company presented each new consumer with an electric iron.

The floors in all of the rooms in the house were covered in linoleum, which, although easy to clean, was very cold to the touch. This problem was partially overcome by placing small carpets, some made from rag clippings, in front of the fireplaces.

All of the fires were fuelled by coal, and it was necessary to have this coal delivered, usually one ton at a time, and carried through the downstairs passage in one hundred-weight bags, to the coal cellar at the rear of the house.

The fire in the downstairs kitchen was lit daily, but it was seldom that any of the other bedroom fires were lit, unless someone was ill and confined to bed. In order to prevent chimney fires, the kitchen chimney had be swept twice a year by a chimney sweep, who had to climb out of a skylight window set into the roof, and scramble across the slates in order to drop his weighted circular brush 'doon the lum'. Meanwhile, he had fixed a large sheet across the mantelpiece in the kitchen in order to catch the falling soot. Apart from a little dust around the fireplace, the only mess that the sweep ever left were his dirty footprints on the linoleum, and these were washed off quite easily.

The rear door of the house, at the end of the long passage that ran from the front to the back, opened onto a large concrete area. In a corner of this area stood the water-closet, which was about four feet square. This contained only a toilet pedestal and a chain-operated cistern, and access to the water-closet could only be gained by going outside of the house in all kinds of weather and also in the dark at night.

On the far side of the concrete area was a two-storey outbuilding, which comprised a gear-loft upstairs and a coal cellar and washing house below. Access to the upstairs loft was gained by going through a small passageway in the ground floor, called the 'through-gang', then up a flight of stone steps at the rear.

The gear-loft (referred to as "the laft") had a wooden floor, two small windows, and its own fireplace. Its main function was as a store for items of fishing gear, which were either too heavy or unsuitable for taking up to the garret. These items included coils of thick tarry rope and 'sculls', the latter being specially shaped baskets for containing the great-lines, known locally as 'gartlins'.

When the self-contained flat on the first floor of the main house was let to summer visitors, make-shift beds could also be made up in the gear-loft as well as in the garret, and this is where some of the more agile members of the family would then sleep. The gear-loft was also a very suitable play area for me, along with some of my pals, during wet or cold weather.

Below the gear-loft, the stone-floored washing-house, which had a small window at its front, contained a coal-fired built-in boiler, with a wooden lid covering the metal tub. A water tap, directly above, was used to fill the boiler, but the only way to get the hot and sometimes boiling water out of the tub was to scoop it out with a metal pail or a large ladle. Other items of equipment stored in the washing-house were a large wooden barrel, and two wooden tubs placed on stands. There was also a mangle for squeezing the water out of the clothes after they had been washed.

Monday was always 'wash day', which required an early rise at six o' clock in the morning, in order to get the boiler filled with water, and the fire lit. After a quick breakfast, all the previous week's dirty clothes and bed-linen would be taken to the wash-house, and sorted out ready for the washing. The water in the boiler would now be scalding hot, and buckets of this water would be lifted over and into the barrel, where a small block of 'Acdo' soap powder would be added.

The clothes in the barrel would then be thumped for several minutes with a large wooden 'dolly'. The dolly was an item of equipment measuring about three feet long, with handles protruding like horns out of the top end, and at the other end there was a large wooden block, carved to form thick wooden prongs on the bottom. Pounding the clothes with the dolly was hard work, but was necessary in order to get the soapy water to achieve its purpose.

Some of the more ingrained items were put into the boiler and boiled until clean. Other items were laid out on boards and scrubbed manually with a hand-brush.

The next stage in the process was to rinse all the soapy water from the clothes, and this was done in the tubs using freshly drawn water. The water then had to be squeezed out of the clothes by putting the smaller items through a hand-wringer, and the larger ones through the mangle.

Then the washing had to be carried through the 'through-gang' and up to the drying-green at the top of the garden, where it was hung out on the clothes-lines to dry in the wind. When dry, the smaller items were ironed, and the larger articles, such as sheets and blankets, were again put through the mangle and folded at each stage, in order to press them into a tidy shape.

On Saturday mornings, the weekly ritual of cleaning the house and windows took place. Everything had to be given special attention, and even the pavement at the front of the house had to be scrubbed and washed down. This ritual was carried out by most of the houses in Cellardyke, and if any of the neighbours were cleaning their windows or scrubbing their pavements at the same time, it became an opportunity to take a five minute break to catch up with any gossip.

When all of this work had reached its completion, it was known as being 'all through'. If any of this outside cleaning work was still being carried out when the neighbours had completed theirs, an observant passer-by would likely make the comment, "Are ye no' through yet?"

On Saturday afternoons, the washing-house became the bath-house, as that was the only place with the privacy required for anyone wishing to take a bath. One of the aforementioned washing tubs was used as a bath, and was placed down onto the cold cement floor for that purpose, but was so small that adults could only sit in the tub with their legs hanging over the side. The tub had to be filled with hot water from the boiler by using a bucket; but emptying presented no problem, as the tub was just tipped up onto the cement floor, and the waste water then ran out of the washing-house door towards the outside drain.

There was a fairly large garden to the rear of the gear-loft, which contained rose bushes and various other flowers, and a vegetable garden, which had four fifteen-foot tall thick wooden posts at each corner, all joined together with two rows of horizontal wooden spars. This framework was referred to as the 'galluses', and this was the gallows on which the nets were hung out to dry. Large hooks situated at either end of the garden were used to secure the ropes that were supporting the drying nets.

Towards the rear of the garden was a section given over to growing raspberries; then came the drying green, with a large flower border on the far side. At the top of the green was a permanent garden seat, which was a favourite retreat for older family members on sunny summer days.

At the farthest end of the garden was a hen-hut, where our hens provided us with fresh eggs.

As the years progressed, certain improvements were implemented and, towards the end of the Second World War, we bought a proper metal bath, which gave us the luxury of being able to stretch out properly. It was loosely installed into the washing-house, but, like its predecessor the wooden tub, had to be filled by taking pails of very hot water from the boiler.

An electric washing machine was bought a few years later, together with a small electric water boiler.

After I left home in 1950 to do my National Service in the army, the downstairs rear bedroom in the main house was converted into a kitchen, and a part of this room was then walled off in order to build a modern bathroom and toilet.

This was indeed a very welcome improvement, as this meant that the days of having to brave the elements in order to visit the toilet in the dead of night were now a thing of the past.

Chapter Four

Schooldays

I was only four years and four months old when I was first sent to Cellardyke School in August, 1935. This was one day that I was not looking forward to, as it was going to take away all of my freedom.

I didn't want to go, as instead of being at the school I had wanted to go with my Dey for our usual daily walk along to Anstruther, and to look at the boats in the harbour.

My Aunt Lizzie took me up to the school to get enrolled that morning, and that presented no problem; but when she left me with the teachers, I decided that I was not having any of this nonsense, so I ran out after her.

She told me that I had to go to school, and I burst into tears. The infant teachers, Miss Elder and Miss Dewar, had seen me make my escape and followed me out, and I was dragged back into the school by the two of them, but not before I had put up a good struggle. On many a later occasion, when my first day at school was being recalled, I was reminded of my antics that morning:

"He kickit the bell oot o' the teacher's haund", was one rather exaggerated reminiscence. It was recalled, however, that it didn't take long for the teachers to gain control, as it was also remarked: "Ah dinna ken whaat they did tae 'im efter they got 'im inside, bit he wis a' richt efter that, an' he nivver shouted or kickit up ony row wi' the teachers ivver again".

I have to agree that, after that first day, and once I had settled down, I was quite happy in being at school. I enjoyed most of the school-work, and did quite well with my lessons. In

Cellardyke parlance, I was considered to be 'faur forrit' (far forward – i.e. very good) at spelling, reading and doing sums.

After the infant classes of Primary One and Primary Two, and when Primaries Four and upwards were reached, there was a system of being seated in the class according to how pupils had performed in the weekly classroom tests, which were held mostly on Friday mornings. I enjoyed the competitive nature of these tests; always striving to get good marks.

The seating arrangements were such that children with the top marks sat in the back row, while the rest of the class were graded forwards until the ones with the lowest marks sat in the front of the class, in front of the teacher's desk. So, every Friday afternoon, after the tests had been marked and the results obtained, there was a noisy flitting of the pupils moving from one desk to another, to where their new places had been allocated for the following week.

Boys and girls were seated separately, with the boys being seated towards one side of the classroom, and the girls towards the other. The seating in most of the classes was by using double seated desks. These desks had a top lid, covering a box compartment underneath, where the books and other items were kept when not required for a particular lesson.

In many of the classrooms, the rows of desks were arranged in tiers, with each tier being a foot or so higher than the row in front. This allowed better visibility for the pupils, who were sitting in the back rows, to see the teacher. I suppose that it also allowed the teacher to keep a better eye on the behaviour of all of those pupils who were sitting towards the rear of the class.

We always had to salute our teachers when going into class, by raising our right hands to touch our foreheads. This ritual was also carried out whenever we met any of our teachers in the street. This compulsory act was considered as showing a mark of respect, but it also gave us a sense of discipline, which did us a lot of good.

As mentioned earlier, the infant teachers were Miss Elder in Primary One and Miss Dewar in Primary Two. Miss Elder was very popular and, while I was in her class, she formed a percussion band, with bells, cymbals, musical triangles, tambourines and drums. I do not know how she managed to put up with the noise, but her pupils enjoyed it immensely.

The Primary Three teacher was Miss Landale, and I think that she was my favourite out of all of the primary teachers. She was great at telling stories, and I believe that she was quite influential in encouraging me to become an enthusiastic reader of books at that time. Miss Landale also taught us country dancing, and I remember the names of two of these dances as being 'Petronella' and 'The Haymakers'.

Miss Helen Brown (who lived next door to us in West Forth Street) was my teacher in Primary Four, and Miss Thomasina Murray (who was a cousin of my grandfather) was my teacher in Primary Five. However, despite having an 'out-of-school' relationship with these two teachers, I did not receive any favours from them.

Mr. David Stewart (popularly known as Stewarty) was the teacher in Primary Six, and he was very popular. He had some sort of physical problem, where he could not turn his head without turning his shoulders. Boys thought that this might be due to a wound inflicted in the Great War, but I am not sure if that really was the reason.

The regular Primary Seven teacher was Miss Lizzie Gardner, and almost the whole of the school lived in dread of her. I was lucky in that I was never really in her class, as I was only there for about an hour each week for music lessons. The reason for this was that CellardykeSchool suddenly had a large increase in the school roll in early 1941, due to many children being evacuated out of the cities, mostly from Edinburgh, in anticipation of these places being bombed by German aeroplanes during the Second World War.

Classes had to be re-arranged because of the influx of evacuees and, with me being one of the younger pupils in my age group, I was kept back for an extra couple of terms in Mr. Stewart's class. However, by the end of the Christmas break, a retired teacher from St. Monans, called Miss Christina Murray, was asked to come out of retirement to help out. She was a fairly quiet soul, and was possibly looking for an easy time, so my final six months at Cellardyke School were much more enjoyable than they would have been had I been living in fear of the dreaded Miss Gardner!

Much of the teaching in some subjects, in particular Geography or Music, was done on a communal chanting basis. For example, in Geography, the teacher would use a long wooden pointer to point to places on a large wall map of Scotland, and each time the pointer hit any place on the map, the class would then have to say, and repeat in unison, the name of the place.

This was so loud that any person walking past the school at the time would hear this chanting taking place, sounding something like: "The Moray Firth – The Moray Firth – The Solway Firth – The Solway Firth – The Firth of Tay – The Firth of Tay", and so on. This teaching method was also used when teaching singing, whereby the teacher, by using her pointer, would indicate a note listed on a large 'Soh-Fah' music scale wall chart. The class then had to sing, again in unison, that correct note on the music scale.

Up to about the end of 1938, all of our written school-work was done on wooden framed slates, which were written on with a slate pencil. From about that time, these slates were to be gradually phased out, but the shortage of paper due to the war, which started in 1939, meant that slates again came back into use for a further year or two. All the pupils had to buy their own slate-pencils, and also provide a small sponge, which was kept wet in a small tin box, for the purpose of washing their slates clean after use.

The fact that these sponges were kept sealed away in a tin caused them, eventually, to smell rather badly. It was considered as a highly amusing (and often played) nasty trick to suddenly ram these smelly pieces of sponge under some unsuspecting pupil's nose.

Some written work still had to be done by using a pen and ink, and the pens required frequent dipping into the inkwells set into the tops of the desks. Every couple of months or so, these inkwells would require washing out, and about three boys would be selected by the teacher to go and do this job in the cloakroom. Without fail, this was an excuse for a 'carry on', with water being thrown or squirted at each other, much of which ended up all over the cloakroom floor. If the teacher caught us at this lark, we would inevitably end up getting a few strokes of the belt, also known as the 'tawse'.

In my opinion, the belt, as a punishment, was thoroughly deserved in such cases. Although weals would sometimes appear on a person's hand for a few hours, the practice of belting for misdemeanours did maintain much of the discipline necessary in school, and kept many of the wrong-doings to a minimum.

However, it was still the practice for the belt to be used as a punishment for some pupils who may have got their sums or spelling wrong; or if their other class-work was not seen as being up to the standards required by the teacher, and I do not think that was fair.

It was a rare event to see any girl getting the belt, as usually they would be in tears before the punishment took place. I never yet saw any weals on a girl's hand or wrist.

Occasionally, a boy would take fright, at the last second, when seeing the belt coming down, and would quickly withdraw his held-out hand. This resulted in the teacher receiving the full impact of the belt onto his or her own leg or knee. The intended recipient of the punishment could then expect to get another extra couple of strokes of the belt. Onlookers in the class had to be careful in that they showed no amusement at this scene, otherwise they might also receive their share of the same punishment.

At the end of every class year, in Primary Five and upwards, book prizes were awarded to the best three boys and best three girls in each class for their school-work. I received First Prize in Primary Six, and Second Prizes in Primaries Five and Seven.

Dress at school was very plain and ordinary, with most of the boys dressed in navy-blue 'Guernseys' (woollen jumpers), which were smaller versions of those worn by the fishermen. All the boys wore short trousers, and I was twelve-years-old before I had my first pair of long trousers, in the form a suit, to be used only as my best Sunday clothes. Most of the short trousers ended up being patched in the seat several times, and usually boys outgrew them before they were considered to be worn out.

My Aunt Lizzie, being a part-time seamstress for Duncan the draper, made most of my short trousers. Exceptions to short trousers, of course, were a pair of dungarees, which every boy wore while playing 'over the rocks' (on the seashore), or when at the harbour. There was not a lot of money about, and consequently clothes were expected to last for quite some time. It has to be said that even in the families who were considered to be 'better off', there were never any pretensions of grandeur in the way that their children were dressed. It would have been very difficult to pick out the children of the schoolteacher, or the banker, for example, from amongst the others, as all the children were clothed in much the same way.

Smartly-dressed wearing short trousers in December 1940

Most of the boys wore a 'sugar-bowl cap' in the winter-time, and some would wear a tie if their jersey had a knitted collar. 'Pixie hats' were considered the latest fashion for the girls, and were worn when the weather was cold.

School went in at 9 am., and came out for dinner (lunch) at 12.45 pm. The pupils then went back in for the afternoon session at 1.45 pm., which lasted until 3.55 pm. Play interval at school was called 'lief-time', which I think is a shortening of 'relief time'. This lasted for about a quarter of an hour, and was held at 11 am every morning.

School meals were unheard of, and nearly all of the children went home for their dinners, the exceptions being the children who lived at some distance, for example on the farms, and who therefore had to bring their 'pieces' with them.

Since I lived only a couple of minutes' walk from the school, it didn't take me long to go home, and after dinner I usually hurried back to school to have half an hour's play before everyone went back into the classrooms. However, on the way back to school, it was a frequent custom for me to go up Rodger Street to 'Wulliemeenies' (Mrs. Martin's shop), and buy a 'lucky bag' for a penny.

These lucky bags usually contained about four sweets, a picture and maybe a metal puzzle. As alternatives, children would buy 'sherbet sookers' or liquorice stalks.

Occasionally, we would buy a few 'transfers', which were pictures that had to be wetted before being rubbed through on to our hands and arms. This delicate ritual occupied much of our remaining play-time until the school went back in for the afternoon.

Chapter Five

Playground Games

When we weren't pre-occupied with sticking transfers on ourselves, or partaking in some other suchlike pastime, our 'lief-time' in the playground was taken up with organised games, some of which were team games that involved almost every child in the school.

To start any game, it had first to be 'cried', and this meant that one boy, or a small group of boys, would stand in a particular corner and, in unison, would chant the name of the game that was to be played. As more boys decided to take part, they would join the instigators, and add their voices to the shouting, until there were sufficient participants to start the game.

The next part of any game was to see who was to be 'It'; or, in other words, who was going to be the player who was first nominated to be the 'chaser' or 'catcher', or have some other responsible position, depending on what game was being played. This was done by lining up all the intended players, and then 'counting out' to decide by process of elimination who 'It' was going to be.

In the process of 'counting out', the person who suggested having the game, and therefore being <u>his</u> game, would tap each person in turn on the shoulder, and say the words of a chant, one word corresponding with each tap. One of the common 'counting out' chants was, "Salt fish and fresh fish are just the same. Trout, trout, trout, you are out". Another chant was "One potato, two potato, three potato, four; five potato, six potato, seven potato, more". In that chant, each intended player would hold up his two fists to be counted. This meant that if there were eight players, the chant had to be gone through sixteen times. More than often, another couple of boys would arrive after the 'counting out' had started, and would ask to join in the game. So, the 'counting out' had to start right from the very beginning again.

More often than not, more of the 'lief-time' was used up in the 'counting out' than in playing the game itself. It was only with a bit of luck that any game ever got started before it was time to march back into class!

These are the games that I remember most fondly:

'Tig' was usually confined to about half a dozen pals, but had to be played dodging in and around the rest of the schoolchildren in the playground, who were likewise occupied with their own games.

'Bools' was the local name for the game of marbles, and it was played with various types of marbles: Clay; Glessies or Steelies. 'High knuckly' was a clever stance taken when throwing the 'bool' from a high position. A decision also had to be made, as to whether the game would either be 'Singles' or 'Ringy'. Singles was played by one 'bool' chasing another across the playground (or along the road!), and 'Ringy' was played by knocking the 'bools' out of a small ring marked out on the earth, or marked out with chalk if it was played on the concrete of the playground.

'Cocky Ross' was usually played in the front playground of the school, and was just virtually a mass charge of about thirty boys across the open area, from one end to the other, with initially one boy in the centre being 'It'. His job was to catch any of the other boys as they barged across, and any boy so caught then became an additional 'It'. The number of 'It's gradually increased in later charges, until the last boy was eventually caught, his last charge being on his own, with all the other boys trying to catch him. This game had more than its usual share of torn clothing.

'Horny' or 'Hornygates' was a variation of Cocky Ross, but the catchers joined hands with each other to gradually build up into a 'gate' across the playground. It was mostly played in the larger playground at the rear of the school, where there was more room for large 'gates' of maybe fifteen boys in the row.

'Relievio' was also similar to 'Cocky Ross', but with two equal-sized teams, and was also played in the larger rear playground. In this game, when a boy was caught, the catcher had to hold on to him and count slowly up to five. That boy was then put in a den, and was out of the game until one of his team was able to put a foot into the den and cry "Relievio". The teams changed over their roles when all of the 'free' side were captured.

'Roonders' was the normal game of Rounders, but could only be played if the playground was fairly empty, thus giving plenty of free space in which to play the game. Occasionally, if a ball had been hit too hard, it may have struck the glass in a school window, and the Headmaster would then ban the game from the playground. However, after a few months, the game would gradually creep back again into our playtime.

'Hocky Dock' was a very dangerous game. Two teams were picked, with about six boys in each. The team losing the toss of a coin had to line themselves up in a row, with one boy standing with his back against the wall, and acting as a 'cushion'. The next boy then stood, with his body bent forwards, and with his head pressed against the cushion's stomach. The third boy, and so on, then stood similarly bent, behind and leaning on the rear of the boy in front, until the team looked like a lengthy camel. The other team then had to do a leap-frog type jump, one at a time, along the length of the camel, until all were seated. Then the team on top had to chant, "Hocky Dock, Hocky Dock, three times over", and repeat this three times, while the team underneath were trying hard to shake off the boys who were mounted on top. If the team underneath collapsed, the whole thing had to take place again, as the team on top were considered to have managed to stay on, and were therefore the winners. If, however, the team underneath stayed intact and managed to shake off any of the team on top, then the team roles were reversed for the next game. Occasionally, some boy would get hurt, and his teacher would get to know about it, with the result that every few months or so, an edict was issued by the Headmaster to state that this game was banned from the playground. However, a few months later……………?

'Katty Batty' was a game that I have never heard of being played anywhere else except in Cellardyke. It consisted of a bat, made from wood taken from a fish-box, and a 'Kat', which was a short piece of wood, about five inches long and one inch square in section, and numbered on each side with the Roman numerals of I to IV (1 to 4). Both ends of the Kat were whittled away to a point. A base was chosen in a corner of the playground and the player who was 'It', stood a few paces from this base, and threw the Kat towards the player in the base, who was wielding the bat. This batsman then hit the Kat with the bat, in order to get it as far away from the base as possible. Wherever the Kat landed, it was examined to see which number was showing on top, and this number then decided the further number of strokes that the batsman would be allowed. Each stroke consisted of striking one of the pointed ends of the Kat, thus making it jump up into the air, where it could then be batted even further away from the base. When the Kat had landed for the final time, the batsman had then to state the number of his shoe-lengths that lay between him and the base. The boy in the middle, who was 'It', then had to agree to this figure, or else challenge the batsman. If the batsman had estimated too high a number, and a challenge was made, he would have to measure the number out, heel to toe in a straight line, usually with another two players, one on either side to support him. A batsman, failing the count, became 'It' for the next game; otherwise it was the batsman with the smallest score who became 'It'. Smaller boys, who usually had much smaller feet, could therefore make higher scores than the bigger boys, but the bigger boys could usually bat the furthest distance. Individual scores were kept as a tally, to ascertain who the overall winner was. Needless to say, the boys who attended CellardykeSchool were exceptionally good at counting and estimating distances.

The rear playground at CellardykeSchool was laid in very even and smooth concrete, with a gentle slope on it. This was ideal for making a slide during frosty weather in the winter time. To make sure that these slides were at their best, most of the boys who lived near the school would go back to the playground in the evening. They would then fill their mouths with water taken from the playground well and spray it on to the area where the slide was to be made.

The freezing temperatures during the night left an icy surface to slide on and, the next morning, everyone who had helped to make the slide arrived early at school in order to have half-an-hour's fun on the well polished slide before the bell rang. Any boys who had not helped during the previous evening had to try to make their own feeble slides from what frost was available on other parts of the playground.

Inevitably, there were always some squabbles in the playground, and these would often end up in a fight between two boys. The cry soon went round the playground that there was a fight on, and every other game stopped in order to make a ring round the rivals, with much cheering on and encouragement being shouted for both combatants. If any contestant was knocked down in the fight, he was always allowed to get back up before any more blows were struck. These blows could be quite hard, and a bleeding nose, a burst lip, or a black eye was common, but it was considered very dishonourable to use one's feet, and I rarely saw any boy being kicked during a fight.

One final playground memory is of a few boys having a conversation, whilst hanging upside-down on the playground perimeter walls, like bats, with their feet anchored safely between the bases of the high railings that were affixed to the top of the walls. This was a common sight to see until the railings were taken away in 1940 to be turned into scrap metal to help with the war effort.

Chapter Six

Street Games and Other Pastimes

When I was a small boy, three of my chums; Bobby Melville, George Doig and John Watson; also lived in West Forth Street, just a few doors away.

As soon as school was finished for the day, I ran home to change into older 'playing clothes', before going straight back out to play with my three chums in West Forth Street.

The clothes we played in comprised of short trousers that were no longer considered good enough for school, and 'Guernsey' woollen jumpers. If it was summer weather, off came our shoes and stockings, and we ran about barefoot. In colder weather, we sometimes wore dungarees or a boiler suit, which helped to give a little bit more protection and warmth, if that was considered necessary. If we were to be playing at the seaside, then a pair of rubber wellington boots kept our feet dry, when playing in the rock-pools.

After dark on a winter night, if the weather was good, there were usually many children playing outside, underneath the gas lamps. These lamps were well spaced out, and therefore, although there seemed to be a concentration of warm yellow light underneath each lamp, there were plenty of fairly dark patches between them. When lit, the gas in the lamps gave off a nice friendly hissing sound.

There was never any traffic about, as hardly anyone in the town owned a car, and lorries or horse-drawn carts were only seen during the day. The buses did not come through the streets of Cellardyke at that time, and were only seen on the main thoroughfare through Anstruther and heading down Rodger Street in order to access the bus stances near the north end of the West Pier.

One of the games played underneath the gas lamps on these traffic-free streets was 'Kick the Can', where an old tin can was kicked down the Wee Wynd, and the person who was 'It' had to go and fetch the can, and replace it, whilst the other players made themselves scarce. This game was actually a form of 'Hide and Seek', and the person who was 'It' had to capture the other players and take them back to the den, which was the area beside the can. However, anybody who had not been spotted, and who could manage to get back to the can un-noticed by the person who was 'It', was at liberty to kick the can again, and thereby release all the 'prisoners' from the den.

Girls who lived close to the Wee Wynd were allowed to join in these games of 'Kick the Can', as we usually needed them to make up enough numbers! At other times we would join them in their skipping rope and jumping rope games.

Another game that the girls played was 'Peevers', known in other parts of the world as Hop-Scotch, and the required playing area was marked out with chalk on the pavement. Boys would often force their way into the girls' game, trying to show off to the girls that they thought themselves to be much superior in their skills.

After it got a bit late, it became time for everyone to go to their homes, and most of the children had brothers or sisters to play indoor games with, before going to bed. With me not having any brothers or sisters, I was occasionally allowed to go to somebody else's house for a little while, or alternatively, they would be allowed to come to our house, but mostly I had to come home alone. That was when my Dey stepped in, and we would play at Dominoes or Draughts until my bedtime.

Before going to bed, I had to have my face, hands and knees washed thoroughly, a job that I was not allowed to do by myself at that early age, probably because I would have missed too much of the dirt accumulated that evening playing games in the street. I hated getting washed!

There was one occasion when a full-scale wooden sword-fight war, which lasted several days, broke out amongst the older boys. The two sides in the conflict were the 'aist-the-tooners' and the 'wast-the-tooners' (meaning those from the 'east of the town' against those from the 'west of the town'). I was one of the younger 'wast-the-tooners', and we were asked to go on sentry duty, and report to the bigger boys if we saw any of the 'enemy' coming into our area. A few of us smaller boys were playing in the park at side of Cellardyke Kirk one evening, just as it was getting dark, when about twenty of the enemy came over the wall from the field which lay to the east. We took to our heels and ran off home.

Games were usually played according to the seasons, and 'bools' would be played at a time when it was not too cold, when it was possible to kneel in comfort on the ground. Sometimes, there were 'internationals', when the Dykers (the Cellardyke laddies) would go off to Pittenweem, around two miles to the west, and challenge the boys there.

Street toys were Girds, Barrows, Hurdies and, later, Tyres. My Gird (a hoop) was made by Ramsay, the blacksmith in Kilrenny, and cost sixpence. It did not have a handle, and had to be 'cawed' (pushed along) by a stick. Most of the streets were laid with 'causey stanes', and the noise of girds rattling across these stones gave out a ringing sound. Eventually, when cars and vans started to become more commonplace within the town, it became easier to pick up an old tyre, and these tyres began to replace the girds.

Another occupation, played by both boys and girls, was in wearing 'Tinny Feet', where we walked about with one foot on top of each of two upturned large syrup tins. These were either tied on above the shoes in shoe-lace fashion, or were held on by hand with loops of string extended upwards to thigh level. With half a dozen children progressing slowly along the street on their tinny feet, the associated clip-clop noise from the cans was tremendous. Walking on wooden stilts, with the steps for the feet being placed about two feet above ground level, also became fashionable for a short time, probably after seeing such being used at a circus or at the cinema.

Every boy in Cellardyke carried a pocket-knife, and by carrying such a knife, we were emulating the customary habits of all the adult fishermen. In addition to their use for cutting rope and twine, these knives were extensively used for whittling away at a piece of box-wood, and soon a scrap piece of wood could become a boat or a revolver to be used in any relevant games. Toys bought specifically for these games were completely unnecessary, as home-made efforts always embodied a little pride, and consequently were considered much better. The knives were never used for wrongful purposes.

Nearly every boy had a barrow, made from a fish box and old pram wheels. With one boy in the barrow, and another boy between the shafts acting as a horse, with a length of rope round his shoulders as make-believe reigns, we played at Roman chariots, and had races along the streets.

From barrows, we progressed to 'hurdies'. These were planks of wood, with a fish box mounted at the rear end, and a fixed pair of wheels underneath that end. At the front end of the plank was another pair of wheels on a swivel, which allowed the 'hurdie' to be steered by a rope, controlled by the person seated in the fish box. It was quite common to find two boys sitting in the box. A sloping hill was all that was necessary for these 'hurdies' to race downhill, and there are plenty of these suitable hills in the roads and wynds in Cellardyke.

A look-out was necessary at the bottoms of the hills, to make sure that there was no other traffic, but any street traffic at that time was a rarity, and there could often be up to half-an-hour after any car or a horse-drawn cart had passed before another came along.

Collecting cigarette cards was another vocation of my young days. These were issued in packets of cigarettes, as a sales promotion gimmick, by the different tobacco companies. In each packet, there would be a picture card, with a short description on its reverse side. The card would be one of a series of fifty, and boys would try to collect the whole set, which could then be mounted into a special book. If we had duplicates of the same card, then this would be swapped with other collectors, in order to obtain a full set.

The names of the different series of cards which I can remember as having collected were 'Wild Flowers', 'Famous Footballers', 'Railway Equipment' and 'Life in the Navy'.

When it was the winter herring season, and before the boats arrived back into the harbour each day from the fishing, there were many fish buyers hanging around the pier and the Post Office at Anstruther, waiting for orders, which either came by telegram, or by telephone to one of the call boxes there. As there were sure to be many smokers hanging around this area awaiting orders, this proved to be a lucrative place for acquiring cigarette cards.

Another winter pastime was sledging, and for this purpose I had a wooden sledge, which was made for me by my Dey. If there had been a good snowfall, I would go with other boys to Castle Hill, which lies to the east of Cellardyke, or over to the Billowness at the west end of Anstruther, and take part in a good bit of sledging. Being winter time, this was mostly after dark, but we could see our way in the poor light as there was always a certain amount of luminosity given out by the snow.

On a more mischievous note, a good snowfall meant a good snowball fight, and throwing a snowball at anyone was considered a fair sport. We always observed a code of honour, though, and never threw snowballs at anyone wearing glasses.

Living in West Forth Street, we were on the route taken by the factory girls from Martin's or Watson's factories, who were on their way to the 'bus stop in Anstruther to catch the 'bus home to Pittenweem or St. Monans. They would walk, arm-in-arm and often singing, along the middle of the street past our houses. If it had been snowing, we were always ready for these girls to run the gauntlet, every night at just after half-past-five. On one particular occasion, however, after having made a good hit on the back of one factory lassie's neck, this girl, called Janey Ritchie, turned the tables and ran after me. She could run faster than I could and, after catching me and getting me down on the ground, she proceeded to rub my face with the snow, and stuff it down my neck. I never threw a snowball at Janey again!

So what became of the three chums with whom I played street games and got up to mischief with during my early childhood days in West Forth Street?

Bobby Melville moved away to live in Edinburgh at an early age. He later became a lawyer with the National Coal Board.

George Doig eventually became a marine engineer, and later joined the Merchant Navy. Sadly, on his first trip, near Australia, he fell down the hold of the cargo ship that he was working on, and was killed.

John Watson, who was my closest pal at that early age, also became a marine engineer, and had his own engineering business locally after serving some time as such in the Merchant Navy.

Chapter Seven

The Kirk and Sunday School

Chalmers Memorial United Free Church in Anstruther

The church which our family attended was Chalmers Memorial United Free Church in Anstruther. Although still referred to locally as the being the 'Free Kirk', all of the United Free Churches had re-united themselves with the established Church of Scotland in 1929.

When I became old enough to go to the Church and the Sunday School, my next door neighbour, Mrs. Ann Dick, had noticed that I had been there, and asked me how I liked going to the Kirk. I replied, "Its a' richt, but I dinna like the minister, Mr. Snadden, because he shouts ower lood".

On Sundays, I always had to dress in my best clothes, and this was a three-piece suit of jacket, trousers and waistcoat. I liked to have a waistcoat with four pockets, which gave me plenty of space to store all my bits and pieces. This best suit was kept for Sundays only, until I was beginning to grow out of it, when it became relegated to second best.

Religion was taken very seriously in all the fishing villages along the Fife coast, and Cellardyke was no exception. As well as attending the 'Free Kirk' and the Sunday School on Sunday mornings, I attended the Baptist Church Sunday School on Sunday afternoons, together with lots of children from all the other churches in Cellardyke and Anstruther.

When I was aged nine, I decided that I did not want to go to Chalmers Church any more, as most of my chums went to Cellardyke Church. So, I was then allowed to go with my Uncle David, his wife Maggie and my cousin Isabel to CellardykeChurch, and to its Sunday School.

However, in 1942, when I was eleven years old, after having become a pupil at the Waid Academy, I went back again to Chalmers, and attended the Bible Class there.

One of the highlights of the summer was the 'jant' (jaunt). These were the annual Sunday School picnics, and since I was attending two Sunday schools, I was allowed to go to both 'jants'. Before the 1939-1945 war came, a lot of these trips were made by train to Boarhills station, a few miles to the south-east of St. Andrews, where a short walk took us to the park at Kenly Green.

The war curtailed these excursions, however, and the picnics were then held nearer home, either at Kilrenny Common or Rennyhill Park, just about a mile or so to the north of Cellardyke. To lend a sense of occasion, we were taken there on a horse-drawn farm cart.

This was the annual occasion for me to have my plimsolls, which we referred to as 'saft shuin', replaced with a new pair, since my previous pair would be worn out. Off we would go, wearing our new shoes, our tin mugs hanging from our belts, looking forward to a happy day. We had team games, and mass participation in jumping ropes, with many adults also joining in. This was followed by the races, all graded into different age groups, and girls separate from boys. Then all the children had to sit in a large circle, and paper bags containing sandwiches, a bun and a cake, were handed out, and our tin mugs were filled with tea.

On Sunday afternoons in the summer-time, when the Sunday schools were also on holiday, it seemed as if almost everybody in Cellardyke made their way to Kilrenny Common, dressed in their best Sabbath finery. Nearly all of the men would be wearing either soft or bowler hats and the women were all decked out in their finest clothes, some in the latest fashion, and quite a bit of 'showing off' took place.

One widespread fashion with women in those days was to have a fox fur, complete with face and paws, draped round their necks, and over their shoulders. Changed days indeed!

There were plenty of seats placed around the Common, but nearly all were filled by early-comers, and many groups of people would just be standing around talking, with the previous week's fishing being the main topic amongst the men.

Meantime, children were allowed to go and have a play, but were instructed quite clearly not to get their Sunday clothes dirty. A game of 'tig' or 'hide and seek' was approved, or else making daisy-chains, or getting a blade of grass between the palms of your hands, and blowing through it, in order to make a whistling sound.

If a birds-nest was discovered, a weekly pilgrimage then ensued to see if the eggs had hatched; followed by further visits to see how the young birds were getting on.

In later years, when we went off on our own, without any supervision from grown-ups, it was still unheard of to wear anything but our Sunday best on the 'Lord's Day'. I am afraid to say, however, that we sometimes went to play in places that were a bit dirty, such as at the boatyard, or climbing trees in the woods, and very often I would be in for a good telling-off if I managed to get a dirty mark on my best clothes.

In the week before Christmas Sunday, there were always the Sunday School soirees, the word 'soiree' being pronounced locally as "sore ee". This party was always a time to be enjoyed, with sandwiches, cakes and tea, then games to be played, such as, 'The Grand Old Duke of York', 'Puir Pussy', 'Musical Chairs', etc.

Afterwards, we would all troop into the church to sing a few carols, before Santa Claus made his entry with a small present for each of the children.

Chapter Eight

Gaun Tae The Picters

Almost every week, on Saturday evenings, I went to one of the cinemas in Anstruther; a ritual which we called the 'gaun tae the picters'.

To begin with, there was only one picture house, called the 'Empire', which had been converted from an old brewery located at the junction of East High Street and Burial Brae. In 1934, a new cinema, the 'Regal' was built at Chrichton Street in West Anstruther.

From the age of seven I was allowed to go to the pictures with my other pals, without the supervision of adults. Children always sat in the front rows, which were the cheapest seats.

In those days before the war, it cost three pence (1½p) for admission to the Empire, and four pence (2p) for admission to the Regal; those prices being in old Imperial money in the days long before decimalisation.

I used to go out on a Saturday night with either five pence or six pence in my pocket. This may seem like a paltry sum by today's standards, but back in the late 1930's it was enough not only to get me in to the pictures, but also enabled me to purchase a penny-worth of sweets or an ice cream on the way to the cinema from Brattesani's, the ice cream and sweet shop in Anstruther's Shore Street. More often than not, I had enough left over to buy a penny-worth of chips on the way home.

At the Empire, the doorman was Robert Watson, who, being the local Town Crier, was known to everybody as 'Bobby Bell', on account of the fact that he used a bell to draw attention to any news he was about to announce.

In order to get the best seats, children would form a queue at the entrance, about a quarter-of-an-hour before the doors were even opened. When Bobby was spotted coming along the street to open the doors, a great cheer rang out!

Tickets were bought at a cubicle just inside the entrance, and Bobby tore these tickets in half as we entered the auditorium. Another cheer went up when the lights went out and the show was ready to start, accompanied by a lot of whistling and stamping of feet.

Brattesani's Ice Cream Shop in Shore Street, Anstruther.

During the performance, there was also usually a lot of noise from the children, either in excitement at a cowboy chase, or in boredom when watching a love scene.

No visit to the pictures was complete without having to suffer the commotion caused by people in the audience having to make visits to the toilet. In order for those seated in the middle of the rows to reach the passage-way on their way to the toilet, everybody in the row was required to stand up, and tip up their seats, so that the person could get past. This commotion was repeated in the opposite direction when the person came back in.

In the winter, we would forego the ice-cream on the way to the cinema, and instead we would buy peanuts, still in their shells, which we only knew by the name of 'monkey-nuts'. When watching the film eating these nuts, their discarded shells always ended up being scattered onto the floor beneath our seats.

By the time someone decided that they needed to visit the toilet, a fair amount of nut-shells would have accumulated on the floor, and these would be crunched about by all the moving feet, causing such a din that the dialogue of the film could not be heard.

Some adults, sitting behind us, would eventually reach the end of their tether because of the turmoil, and would call out for silence. Bobby Bell would then hurry down to the front rows, where the culprits who had dropped the nut-shells were seated, and shine his torch in all our faces, shouting, "Ah'll pit ye a' oot!".

If there had been a good film on, this dictated the subject to be discussed on the way home, and also prompted which games were to be played during the following weeks.

If we had watched a good pirate film, then you could be sure that wooden swords would be dragged out of the toy-boxes, and a game of Pirates would be the order, with all the associated swashbuckling and intricate footwork necessary to simulate a sword-fight.

A good cowboy film had us playing at Cowboys and Indians, where imaginary reins were held in front of us with one hand, whilst the other hand slapped one of our hips. At the same time our feet would scuff a rhythmic beat on the ground, in imitation of a horse trotting along the street.

One boy, Jimmy Mitchell, who lived just across the street from the Empire, went one better. Jimmy always turned up at a cowboy film wearing his cowboy suit, complete with gun and holster, and when the 'goodies' were needing any help, Jimmy would point his gun at the 'baddies', and shoot away at them, while making the vocal sound of bullets being fired!

Sadly, there are no cinemas left in Anstruther today. The Empire was first to close its doors, in the late 1950's, and is now used for storage. The Regal struggled to remain open during the early 1970's, and eventually closed in 1972. After lying empty for several years, it was eventually demolished and replaced by new housing.

Chapter Nine

Seasonal Ploys

A busy scene at AnstrutherHarbour during the Winter herring season, with fish boxes piled up high on 'The Folly'.

From the middle of January until the middle of March, it was the Winter Herring season at the East Neuk fishing ports, and Anstruther was a hive of activity.

The fish-boxes would arrive at the harbour in time for the start of the season, and were stacked about twelve-feet high all along the Folly (the name given to a wide quay that stretched along the north side of the inner harbour, opposite the shops in Shore Street), and down the middle pier.

Because it was winter, the sun was low over the horizon, and very little sunlight managed to get through into Shore Street, due to the height of these stacks. To us boys, the boxes were seen as giant building blocks, which were light enough in weight to allow them to be easily lifted and moved around.

We built caves into the stacks of boxes, with some cunningly contrived entrances with trap-doors, and tunnels that went on for many yards, eventually opening into small 'rooms' inside.

The floors of these 'caves' were made by turning the boxes upside down, and roofs were created by withdrawing a box slightly along the side walls of the tunnels, thus making a narrow ledge, which then supported a few boxes above. Some of these caves were works of art, both in their construction and concealment, and often the fish buyer, arriving at his stance of fish-boxes, would not realise that we were hiding in them. Sometimes, however, we were discovered, and had to run over the top of the stack and climb down the other side to get away. If we were caught, it was a certainty that we would receive a kick from the buyer's hobnailed boot on our backsides, but we never went home to tell about this, or we would also have been in trouble at home.

When the herring were being transferred by derrick, from a boat's hold, up onto the pier, there were always a few that would slip off from the top of the basket, as it landed on the pier. It was considered fair game that we boys could dash in, retrieve these dropped herring, and carry them off with our fingers pushed through their gills, or else threaded together with a piece of string.

We then went around the houses in the town, selling the fish for a penny each and, one night, I made a good sale at Dr. Wilson's house. The following evening I was a bit later doing my rounds, and when I could not find anybody to buy my herring, I thought I would try Dr. Wilson again. Of course, he did not want them again so soon, and as it was no use trying anywhere else, I left the herrings lying in his garden. He knew that it was me who had left them, and when he next saw me in the street, he stopped his car and said that he "had a crow to pick with me", then proceeded to give me a good telling off. I had lost a good customer.

On Saturdays, the herring fleet stayed in port, and a general scrubbing down and clean-up of the boats would take place. All the fish-scales and other waste would be hosed overboard, and the wheel-house windows would be washed clean to remove any dried-on salt spray. Boys were always welcome aboard the boats to help in this work, and our remuneration was to collect the numerous empty jam jars and lemonade bottles which were on board, and return them to the shops. A penny deposit was gleaned on each item, and this money was immediately spent on ice-cream, sweets or more lemonade.

The empty bottles and jars were then sent back to the various jam and lemonade factories for re-use, and the procedure was a very efficient form of re-cycling, as none were ever thrown away to become dangerous litter.

Whenever the Easter school holidays arrived, it was time to spend a lot more time outdoors, and usually we had one or two picnics around that time. In a group of about six boys, we would set off with our 'pieces' and a bottle of lemonade and head for either Kilrenny Common, Innergellie Woods, Caiplie Beach or Caiplie Coves. We would be away from about mid-morning until tea-time.

On one of these trips to the Coves, we decided to see how far we could get into the Piper's Hole, where as local legend supposes, a piper went in playing his bagpipes and was never seen again. This tunnel, which is very low at its entrance, is said to have, at one time, carried on inland, re-appearing behind the fireplace at Barnsmuir farmhouse, and was formerly used by smugglers. As we were going along the tunnel, which was very dark inside, we heard a noise, and saw two green spots of light coming towards us. Thinking it was the ghost of the Piper, we turned around and scrambled out as quickly as we could, shouting and yelling with fright. The green spots turned out to be the light reflected in the eyes of my pal Jimmy Woodward's black Labrador dog, 'Glen', which nobody had noticed going into the tunnel before us!

The summer time saw an influx to the town of visitors and holiday-makers, who would arrive from Edinburgh, Glasgow, Paisley or the Central Belt in their hundreds, by train, on a Saturday. Very few came by bus, and almost none came by car. Arriving at the railway station, some were confronted with a long walk to Cellardyke, where they had taken rooms. They generally had large and heavy suitcases, and the prospect of carrying these for up to a mile daunted them. There was only one taxi in operation, and this was owned by the Commercial Hotel and driven by 'Andra' Carstairs.

Equipped with suitable barrows, boys would wait for the trains to arrive. Andra glowered at us barrow-owners, as we were his opposition, and before the train came in, he would tell us to get away to the end of the road, saying that he had the exclusive rights to operate from the station. At least, that was what he claimed! As soon as he was away with his first lot of passengers, we moved back along beside the waiting crowds, and came to their rescue. A call of "Carry your bag, Mister" was enough to sell our services, and so we escorted them to their rooms. We never made a set charge; we just hoped that we would receive a good tip, and were usually rewarded with a sixpence. That was considered a fair price all round, and everybody was happy. However, I do remember one man who got me to take his cases all the way to Dove Street, at the far end of Cellardyke, before handing over a measly two pence!

Each year, in the second week of August, the Lammas Fair occurs in St. Andrews. This fair was derived from an agricultural and trade market, and has taken place there for hundreds of years. It was always referred to by the Dykers as the 'St. Awndry's Market', and most families, who had young children, made an effort to get there. By the time of my childhood, the fair had lessened into a collection of amusement shows, although there were still a few unusual sideshows, where artistes showed exhibitions of strength or ingenuity. There would often be someone who would ask to be tied up either by ropes or by chains, and he would then struggle around for quite some time, while endeavouring to get free. Another instance is that of a strong man, who would lie face-up on the ground with a large boulder placed across his belly, and would invite his co-partner to smash the boulder into smithereens with a sledge-hammer. Meanwhile, a collecting tin was passed around the spectators.

The L.N.E.R. Railway Company always ran cheap excursions to St.Andrews to coincide with the Market and, as a small child, I was taken there by my grandfather. We did not spend much money, and I would have perhaps been allowed just one go on a roundabout, and also a few tries at 'roll-the-penny' or 'hoop-la'. However, no trip to the market was complete without buying a sugar pig. This pink-coloured treat would be taken home and eaten, just a little each day over the space of a week, to remind me of my trip to the market.

In the autumn, when the chestnuts were ready on the trees, it was the time to play 'conkers'. First of all, the chestnuts had to be obtained, and there were not many of these trees around. Some were located at the side of the main road to Crail at Cornceres Farm, or on the Innergellie estate; or sometimes a bike ride away on the Colinsburgh Straights.

It was no use waiting for the chestnuts to fall, as other boys would have claimed them by that time. Always impatient for getting the chestnuts, we had to knock them down by throwing stout pieces of tree branches up into the trees. These pieces of wood were always traditionally referred to as 'cudgels'. Once we had obtained enough chestnuts, a hole would be bored through each one, before being threaded on to a strong piece of string.

For a few weeks, a string of chestnuts was then part of the contents of every boy's pocket, and the entire school playtime and the journey home from school was occupied with playing at 'conkers'. A score was kept of the number of opponent's chestnuts destroyed, and that was toted up against a particularly good chestnut. When that one also became battered and eventually destroyed, its score was transferred to the new winner.

Kite-flying was another occupation that was very popular when the weather was right. It was always best in autumn, on a bright day with a good breeze. This period was considered as the most suitable time, because the best venue for flying the kites was generally a stubble field, which had plenty of space available after the farmer had finished his corn harvest. The kites were home-made simple affairs, constructed from brown paper glued across a frame made from small canes and string. The counter-weights were made by tying handfuls of grass to the tail string, and this was where skill was required in calculating the correct amount of balance for the strength of the wind on any particular day.

At Halloween, every youngster would go 'guising'. I would dress up for the occasion and, in order to hide my identity, I would have some soot from the chimney rubbed onto my face. I would then visit the homes of relatives, friends or neighbours, and sing a song and tell a story, for which I was rewarded with a penny or so for my efforts.

Another tradition, carried out on the last day of the year, was known in Cellardyke, as 'Cake Day', and on this day we would go round the houses of relatives, friends and neighbours, and chant the following verse: "Ma feets cauld, ma shuins thin, so gie's ma cakes an' let me rin!"

Mostly, it was apples or oranges, which we were given as 'cakes', but sometimes we were given a small round shortbread, which was decorated with iced lettering on top with words such as 'Happy New Year' or 'Good Luck'.

Chapter Ten

Pre-War Memories

Even before our house became connected to mains electricity, we were fortunate enough to have one of the first radios in our street. These radios were always referred to as 'wirelesses', and ours was a home-made affair, built by my Uncle George, with the assistance of his friend Eck Smith, who was a cabinet maker.

Both were very friendly with Tammy Robertson, a shoe-maker to trade, who had his own business in Cunzie Street in Anstruther, but who was also a radio enthusiast and experimented with different wireless kits.

George built a substantial cabinet which was large enough to stand on the floor, into which the wireless unit, assembled by Tammy Robertson, was fitted. The electricity necessary to drive the wireless was obtained from a 120 volt high tension battery and a 6 volt low tension wet acid accumulator which, after a few weeks or so of being in use for only an hour or two each day, had to be taken to either Tammy Robertson's or John Heininen's for recharging.

It was a common sight at that time to see people carrying their accumulators to, or from, these shops in Anstruther for that purpose. Great care had to be taken in carrying the accumulators, since any acid splash would burn a hole into a person's clothes.

When I was old enough, it was my job to make the journey, carrying the accumulator, and I liked to take it John Heininen, a native of Finland, who had married a local girl before settling in the area. John, who spoke with what I considered to be a funny accent due to his origins, made his living from running a bicycle repair shop and, if I showed any interest in what he was working on when I visited the shop, he always took the time to explain his task.

Our wireless was used very sparingly, in order to be economical with the accumulator, but my grandparents listened to all of the daily news broadcasts, and also to any religious programmes, if these were being broadcast.

Silence from everybody else in the house was also expected whilst Uncle George listened to Henry Hall, his favourite band, when they played their weekly spot. My Uncle Tom bought a mains-driven radio for the house around 1940, to replace the battery driven one.

The Easter holidays were the time to start the 'tinney-fire' season down at the seaside. These were small fires which were made inside a small tin; the best container for a tinney fire being an empty 2lb. treacle or syrup tin, which was nice and strong. A hole of about one inch square was cut out through its side, down by the base, in order to provide a through-flow of air. A small fire was then lit inside the tin, and it was fuelled with small pieces of coal. This coal was readily found along the shore, where household ashes, some only partly burnt, had been dumped over the garden walls.

The most popular venue for making tinney-fires was at the Craignoon Skelly, a rock formation on the seashore near Cellardyke Harbour; its elevated and windy situation being ideal for this pastime. Other good sites were the 'Broken Skelly' and the 'Billy Andra' skellies.

A supply of 'wulks' (whelks) and 'lempits' (limpets) would be gathered from the rock-pools, and also a hunt would be made for a clean tin can, in which the wulks would be boiled. A 'Nairn's Floor Polish' tin lid was found to be ideal for roasting the limpets.

Over these tinney fires we would then cook the wulks or lempits. The wulks would have to be ceremoniously brought to the boil five times, and the shells of the lempits would have to be jumping off the tin lid before they were considered ready for eating. A pin was necessary to pick the flesh out of the wulks.

A more sophisticated meal was to be had if we brought potatoes to cook. These were cut up roughly into half inch cubes, and boiled in sea water, so no additional salt was necessary. An even better ploy was to get some fat and fry the potatoes to make chips. The number of chips was more important than the size, so the potato was cut up very small so as to make lots of very tiny chips.

If the fire had been a communal effort, then the bunch of boys who had helped would sit in a circle round the fire, and the chips would be handed out one at a time, until they were finished. It then became time for another fry up!

Gathering and selling a quantity of wulks to a local fishmonger was a good way of making money, providing they were large enough in size. Armed with a metal pail, we would scour the rocks on the seashore and gather as many as we could, dreaming of the fortunes that were about to come into our possession.

Then, with our pails full to the brim, we would struggle over the rocks, and up the steep steps onto the streets. With arms tired from all the carrying, the effort still had to be made to get the wulks along to Joe Smith in East Green, who was the dealer for this particular kind of shell-fish.

After answering the knock at his door, he would slowly accompany us, in complete silence, along the street to his work premises. In the shed, he would then tip our pails individually into the biggest pail that I have ever seen. This pail was called a cog pail, and it made the amount of whelks that had been in our pails look very small indeed. Then he would whistle away to himself for a few moments, deep in thought, before making the great pronouncement, "Fower pence"! On the long trek from the seaside, I had calculated that mine were worth at least a shilling. No wonder every boy always referred to him as 'Miser Joe'.

Depending on the state of the tide, fishing for crabs from the various skellies was great fun, using the flesh of a limpet, tied to the end of a piece of string, as bait. We would then keep the crabs fresh by storing them in large tins or buckets, filled with sea water. After each boy had caught sufficient crabs, they were carried up to the streets, where a good flat surface could be found, and we would then set the crabs down in a line, so as to have crab race.

We would also go 'speeting' for flounders in 'The Run' or in the 'Fluke Dub'. A large cod hook was straightened out, and then lashed on to the end of a cane. This made a suitable spear for throwing at any fish swimming past, but I cannot remember ever catching one that was of a decent size, and worthy of taking home to eat.

Inevitably, with so much activity at the seaside amongst youngsters, someone would trip over a rock, or slip on a patch of seaweed, and would fall into a large 'dub' (puddle). It was a common sight to see a boy making his way up the steps from the seaside on his way home with all his clothes soaking wet. On being asked what had happened by a passer-by, he would give the sometimes tearful answer, "Ah've fa'in in!"; the tears no doubt in anticipation of the row that awaited him at home.

As soon as the school summer holidays arrived, shoes came off and every youngster went around barefoot, except on Sundays. Making our way to the seaside or to the beach at Anstruther harbour on a hot summer's day meant running the risk of stepping into some melted tar from the roads, and what a mess that did make! We never dared go into our houses with such a mess, so somebody had to bring out some butter to slacken the tar, and water to wash our feet afterwards.

For more serious rod and line fishing, I would go with friends to the end of the east pier at Anstruther, and fish for flounders, using lugworm for bait. Having established our berths on the pier, any later arrival who had plans to start fishing close beside any of us, was told "First Cuts"; which was a way of ritually pronouncing to the newcomer that, due to the lack of space, if any 'fankle' (tangle) occurred between the lines after casting then the holder of the 'First Cuts' title had the right to cut the other persons line in order to extricate his own, assuming, of course, that the fankle was bad enough to necessitate this action.

Sailing boats in the large dubs at the seaside was another occupation. There were many model steam drifters and sailing boats used in this game, and a lot of these had working derricks to unload the pretended catch.

The boats were towed along on a length of string and, if the string was connected to the boat a little way along the side from the bow, the boat, when pulled, would tend to move through the water away from the shore. We always called this point on the side of the boat the 'take'.

In our vivid imaginations, we would pretend that our boats were returning from the fishing grounds, and a chunk of green seaweed was placed on their decks as a substitute for the catch.

On other days, we would make boats shaped from flat pieces of wood obtained from a broken fish box, which were about a foot in length. A rough mast would be wedged into a groove on the deck, and a piece of newspaper would be mounted as the sail. These craft were known as 'skifties', and races would be held. Sometimes we would misjudge the direction of the wind, and the skifties would then all sail out to sea. No great loss, however, as another day would mean another boat.

When playing at Anstruther beach, we often made boat shapes and sails out of newspaper, and put a little sand in the bottom for ballast. In an off-shore wind, we would set these off towards the harbour mouth, and the competition was to see how far these paper boats could go before sinking.

For my eighth birthday I was given a model 'Fifie' (a traditional sail-powered fishing boat), which was made by Lock Horsburgh, the brother of my Auntie Jess. It was a full working model, complete with sails, and named 'Boy Alex.', after myself. It was given the registration number KY 439, as my birthday that year was in the fourth month of 1939.

I was so proud of my model Fifie that, for a while, I would not take it to the seaside to sail it in the rock pools on the shore, as I was afraid it could easily be scratched or damaged. Instead, I took it along to safer waters of the Cardinal Steps Bathing Pool at the east end of Cellardyke, where it could be sailed safely if no bathers were in attendance.

I sometimes went out for a sail in a real sailing boat. This was in the 'Ivy', a small boat in which a father and son, both called Peter Smith, went about their business as creel fishermen, fishing for partans (brown edible crabs) and lobsters.

I think that the 'Ivy' was about twenty feet long, and was driven by a lug-sail. For most of the time, however, as the creels were set in amongst the rocks, she was simply powered by oars. Peter, senior, was well-known as the 'Fisherman Poet of Cellardyke', and books of his poems were first published in the early 1950's.

Young Peter Smith, the son of 'Poetry Peter', became a schoolteacher in mathematics at the Waid Academy, and also had a book published, 'The Lammas Drave and the Winter Herring', giving an account of the herring fishing at Anstruther over the years. In this book, there is a photograph of the Ivy sailing into Anstruther harbour, and I am the small boy who is seen on board the vessel, wearing a white shirt.

As we got older, we progressed to making fish-box rafts. These were usually made with about three fish-boxes nailed together, and had a shaped bow built on. The boxes were filled with net corks, most of which were to be found along the shoreline at the high water mark. Also, if available, some large sealed tins were included for buoyancy.

We made paddles for these rafts, and played on them amongst the rocks a few yards offshore. The rafts were very heavy and cumbersome in the water, however, and moved very slowly.

We would frequently fish from them, and some bigger boys would occasionally go out quite a distance from the shore, onto the open sea. This foolhardy behaviour sometimes necessitated their rescue, as on a strong tide they could not paddle fast enough against the current in order to get back to the shore.

In the summer of 1939 I learned to swim. Before this I was rarely out of the water if it was a good day, and usually went in for a bathe at Anstruther harbour beach, but could only wade out so far and not go 'out of my depth'.

On one particular day, however, I went along to Cellardyke Bathing Pool, which was referred to locally as 'The Pond'. I was bathing with Bobby Parker, who was a few months younger than me, and already a good swimmer. We were in a convenient depth of water, about three feet deep, when he asked me why I was not swimming, and I answered that I could not swim.

He said that it was easy, and showed me what to do with my arms and legs. I decided to have a go, and within a few minutes I had mastered the technique. Swimming became one of my great interests from then on. However, I always preferred the harbour at Anstruther for my swimming, probably because it cost nothing to swim there, and we would throw ourselves off the pier into the much deeper water when the tide was in.

Even when the tide was out, we were still able to swim at the outer end of the East pier, where we ran and jumped out over the end for the big drop into the water, usually yelling some slogan, or some popular lines from a film currently showing at the local cinema. Stout wooden planks, 'borrowed' from the boatyard, were wedged into the handrails at the top of the gangway ladders on the piers, and these became our spring boards. If the tide was low, these same boards became our boats in the shallow water of the outer harbour, when we lay along the top of them, using our arms and hands for paddles.

Stone-throwing was a harmless occupation at the seaside, and boys would line up scores of tin cans along the top of the sewage pipes, then have a competition to see who could knock down the most tin cans. Powerful catapults, made from old rubber car tyre inner tubes and the natural forks of the branches of small trees, were also used for this.

While at Sunday school, I learned the story of Goliath being slain by David, in using a sling. This prompted me to make a sling, using the tongue of a discarded shoe, shaped in order to hold the stone, attached to string cords about three feet long. With plenty stones of a perfect size being available at the seaside, I became quite proficient at using my sling, and could make the stones go for a considerable distance, much further than what could be achieved by using a catapult.

An old abandoned salmon cobble lay on the sand above the high water mark at the road entrance to the beach in the outer harbour at Anstruther, and it was often partly filled up with windblown sand. This cobble became the focal point and den for many of the games played on the beach.

One boy, a few years older than myself, named William Muir, or in Dyker language, 'Wullie Mair', on hearing about 'The Black Hole of Calcutta' in a history lesson at school, decided to invent a new game. This game was about being in prison, and the salmon cobble was used as such. The prisoners were considered to be locked up when they were in the very front of the boat, between the front seat and the bow, and there was no escape from there. The warders allowed a few prisoners at a time to come out into the after end of the boat, and the task of these prisoners was to scoop the sand out over the side with their hands. When the sand became nearly all scooped out, the prisoners were ordered outside the boat where they then had to scoop it all back in again.

According to the rules of the game, when the prisoners were outside the boat was when escapes could take place, but the warders were armed with small stones and threw these, one at a time, at anybody attempting to escape. If you got away before a stone hit you, then you were considered to have made a good escape, and you ran off towards the nearby boatyard, with its multitude of hiding places. However, there were roving warders moving around the area, and it was their job to try and recapture you by throwing their small stones at you.

This game was very popular for a few years, and I think that it finally ceased to exist when the cobble fell apart and disintegrated.

In his fifth year at the WaidAcademy, Wullie was nominated by his classmates to be awarded the prize for being the most popular pupil in that year. Later, he emigrated to New Zealand, but sadly lost his life when a fishing boat, of which he was the skipper, foundered in a storm.

Another significant event that occurred in the years leading up to the Second World War was when, as an eight-year-old, I joined the 'Wolf Cubs', when they were being re-formed at Cellardyke School. Later, the pack was transferred to meet in the Drill Hall, in Anstruther. The pack was run by Jimmy Hodge, and I learned to tie all different kinds of knots, which was a skill that became very useful to me in later pastimes. I stayed with the Cubs until I was eleven, and enjoyed going to the weekly meetings.

I wore their uniform of a green sugar-bowl cap, segmented off with yellow piping, and a neckerchief, which was fastened by a 'woggle'. The jerseys were of different colours, probably because nobody had the money available to buy the special green jerseys that cubs would normally wear. I gained several stars and badge awards, which were then sewn on to my jersey.

While in the cubs, we had Halloween parties each year, and a popular game we played was 'dookin' for aipples', where we tried to get our teeth into the fruits which were floating in a tin bath full of cold water. Another traditional contest was to try to spear the floating apples with a fork dropped from our mouths.

A rather messy game played at this time was to eat a 'treacle piece', which was suspended on a piece of string, while our hands were tied behind our backs. The treacle had been spread on to the slice of bread quite generously, and everybody taking part finished up with quite a mess on their faces; some also getting treacle on their clothes and in their hair, caused by the pieces swinging about.

These are the memories of my childhood in the years just before the outbreak of the Second World War in September 1939. I didn't know it at the time, but childhood memories of a very different kind lay just around the corner.

Chapter Eleven

The Outbreak of War

On the morning of Sunday, 3rd September, 1939, I was occupying my usual pew in Cellardyke Church, when the beadle, Peter Muir, came in during the service, and spoke to the minister, the Rev. James Lee. The minister then made the announcement, from the pulpit, to say that war had been declared between Britain and Germany. He immediately brought the service to a close, and we all made our way home, fearful of what lay ahead.

This war was to change our lives in many ways. Although we would still go out to play with our chums, the games were now changed. As a result of the propaganda that gradually infiltrated our everyday lives, the cinemas now showed war films, which proved to be very popular with us youngsters. After having watched a good film, the characters in our games were now soldiers, sailors or airmen; gone were the cowboys and pirates! If a war film was exceptionally good, boys would often remain in the cinema, so that they could watch 'the big film' all over again.

The war caused a lot of shortages in items that had formerly been imported into the country from abroad. This scarcity was especially felt amongst some particular forms of food. One item that disappeared completely was the banana; just a few months into the conflict they disappeared from the shops, and were never seen again until after the war was over. Another commodity which was scarce was sugar, and this in turn affected many other foods, such as sweets and chocolate.

By early 1940, supplies were so meagre that, on Saturdays, large queues formed outside any shops which sold confectionery. During these times of shortage, I would often stand in one of these queues, for maybe twenty minutes or so, for a bar of very plain chocolate. Leaving one shop, people would then go and stand in the queue at another shop, often to be told that all of that week's supply had already been sold out.

Of course, many of these shopkeepers kept their supply hidden under the counter, and would sell only to their 'special customers' when nobody else was around to see!

Proper rationing came in later, and coupons had to be handed over to the shopkeeper from a ration book, in order to get any of these very scarce items, which was a much better way of making sure that everybody got their fair share. Tea, sugar, butter, butcher meat and confectionery were all put on the ration scheme, as well as clothing. Even eggs became fairly scarce, but these were substituted by packets of processed egg powder. Orange juice was made available only for toddlers.

As stated in an earlier chapter, during the summer months in the years before the war the upstairs flat in our house was let to summer visitors. The same families would come to us every year; the Christies from Edinburgh for the Edinburgh fortnight, which was the first fortnight of July; and the Sproulls, who came from Glasgow for the Glasgow Fair, which was during the second fortnight of that month.

After the outbreak of war, these families still came to Cellardyke during the summer, but the Christie children had now grown up, and the two available rooms were not enough to allow the necessary privacy for a grown up mixed family, therefore they found other accommodation.

Mr. and Mrs. Christie, however, always made a point of visiting my grandparents when they were in Cellardyke, and exchanged social niceties. Mr. Christie was a very heavily built man, and worked in the office of the L.N.E.R. at Waverley station in Edinburgh. He had realised that, because of the impending scarcity of chocolate, the vending machines on the station platforms would soon become obsolete. With this in mind, and armed with a handful of penny coins, he went round all the machines and bought as many two-penny bars of Cadbury's milk chocolate as he could.

He decided to put a few aside for giving to me when he next came to visit us in Cellardyke, a kind gesture that I appreciated very much. Although I shared my good luck with other members of the family, I still managed to make my present last for several weeks!

Because of the shortage of sugar, farmers were encouraged to grow sugar beet, which could then be processed into granulated sugar. It became a regular activity for boys, if going for a walk along a country road, to nip into a field for one of these beets. By using knives to scrape away and clean the surface of the beet, they would then cut it up into small cubes, and this became a substitute for sweets.

One of the first air raids of the war took place over the Firth of Forth, when German planes tried to bomb the Navy Base and Dockyard at Rosyth. On my way home from school, I went down to the seaside to watch the enemy planes being chased by the RAF fighters, and one German bomber was brought down into the sea to the south-east of Crail.

Because gas was a weapon that was expected to be used by the Germans against the civilian population, everybody was issued with a gas mask, and these had to be carried constantly. The masks were kept in cardboard boxes, and to protect the box from the rain and dust, I was given a yellow oilskin outer cover with a shoulder strap, which was made by my mother at the local factory. My name was written on the outside, so that I would know which mask was mine, because at school all of these boxes were laid alongside a wall whilst we had our play, and every box looked the same.

Fearful of being bombed at night by the German planes, who it was thought could use the lights from the towns and villages as a guide, the 'Blackout' was introduced. This meant that all street lamps were to be extinguished until the war was over. All of the house windows had to be screened off from dusk until dawn, to make sure that no chinks of light escaped through them. Cars, buses and even bicycles had to have reduced lighting, with the light from their lamps being reduced to a minimum by having special attachments fitted.

In our house, we had large black felt screens, which were fitted every evening across the windows of the downstairs rooms, and also in the bedrooms. Lights were not allowed in the passages or in the garret or attic. If there was no moonlight, then it was very dark in the streets, and electric torches became very popular, but their use was also very restricted. People walked in the middle of the road, in order to avoid falling off the kerbs.

If the weather was not overcast, and if you looked up, it was possible to just make out the outline of the houses against the starlit sky. Often, this faint outline was the only means that people had to help guide them along the road.

Much of the stepping on and off the pavements was done by feeling for the kerb with your foot. In streets such as Rodger Street, in Cellardyke, all of the houses had entrances, which looked the same in both size and style, and in trying to reach their own homes, people had to feel for, and count their way along the gateway entrances in the low walls adjacent to the public footpath. When you came to the house that you were looking for, you then had to feel for the door-handle. There were many instances of people making mistakes in their counting, which resulted in them entering into someone else's house!

Tom Boyter's chip shop closed down during the war, and only Cargill's chip shop at the east end of James Street remained open. With food being scarce and rationed, going to the chip shop at night was sometimes necessary if there was no food in the house, as restaurants were relatively free from rationing restrictions.

Bill Cargill, the chip shop owner, was a small man, but his wife Mima made up for him with her size. There was not much room in the shop, but it was always packed out, with queues forming through the blackout curtains and out into the street. To wait an hour for your turn to be served was quite normal. This became the social event of the day, of course, and it was here that everybody learned all the town gossip. Mima obviously enjoyed every minute of it.

Most of the local steam drifters and larger motor boats were taken away for war service, and the younger fishermen, if they had not already been conscripted into the navy, went with the boats.

The older fishermen, who had stayed behind, looked for and found some older boats, which were considered unsuitable for war service, and brought these back into use, so as to provide a means of continuing the fishing industry.

In the early spring of 1940, at the age of nine, I was fortunate enough to be taken on a trip on one of these old fishing boats, to fish for herring off the Fife coast, along with a few visiting boats who had joined in with the local fleet. The boat I was on was the Berwick-on-Tweed registered 'Pursuit' from Eyemouth; an old sailing 'Fifie', measuring about 65 feet in length, which had been converted from a traditional sailing craft to be powered by a paraffin engine. This engine was mounted in the middle of the cabin, without any dividing wall between the engine and the living quarters of the crew.

The 'Pursuit' had been due to be scrapped, but was resurrected to take the place in the local fishing fleet of the steam drifter, 'Adoration' which had been commandeered for war service. The crew, all Eyemouth men, were mainly in their late fifties and early sixties, and were considered too old for military service. The skipper was Geordie Cowe, and one of the crew was Bill Paterson; both of whom were married to nieces of my grandmother, Jane Swanston.

We left Anstruther harbour in the early evening, and the drift nets were cast before darkness fell. After a few hours or so, the nets were hauled back on board, but the herring proved to be very scarce on that occasion. I have, however, one abiding memory of that fishing trip.

The cook was an old man called Peter, who was very friendly, and he told me that he had a small farm with a couple of cows, a few sheep and some hens. I was fascinated with his stories about his farm, and he said that I would have to go and stay on his farm, when the school holidays came round, and that I would have to help him feed the animals. A few years later, Geordie Cowe informed me that the story about the farm was pure fiction, and that the crew had delighted in seeing me fall for the deception.

None of my uncles were called up into the forces, but nevertheless all of them were very much associated with the war effort. As fishermen, the maritime skills of my Uncles Willie, David and Tam were required to man the requisitioned fishing boats, which then became tenders for the Navy ships at various bases around Britain.

Uncle Willie became the skipper of an M.F.V. at Rosyth, and he continued to work there for many years after the war, until he died in 1959. Uncle David eventually joined the Royal Navy Reserve, and became a Petty Officer, stationed in the south of England.

Uncle Tam worked on the tenders at Scapa Flow in the Orkney Islands, Greenock and Methil. While he was at Scapa Flow, Tam was on the crew of the Cellardyke boat 'Royal Sovereign', but as there was a battleship with that same name, the Cellardyke boat's name had to be changed to 'Cumulus', in order to avoid any confusion.

The crew of the 'Star of Hope', with Uncle Tam leaning on the wheelhouse and Uncle David mending nets in the background.

When a German submarine sneaked into Scapa Flow and sank the battleship 'Royal Oak', the Cumulus was one of the first boats to help in the rescue of some of the few sailors who had managed to swim away from the sinking ship. Together with the rest of the crew of the Cumulus, Tam received a letter of thanks from the Admiral in charge of Scapa Flow, Sir Max Horton.

My Uncle George was not a fisherman, but was employed as joiner at Miller's boatyard in St. Monans. He also became involved in the war effort, however, as Miller's built motor launches for the Royal Navy. In the later years of the war, his employment took him south to the Thames, where he helped with the construction of the Mulberry harbour; the floating dock system that was used in Normandy after the D-Day invasion of France.

During the summer of 1940, I went to Edinburgh with my Aunt Lizzie, to stay for a long weekend with her cousin Charles Marr, his wife Jeannie and their two daughters, Rina and Corine. This was the first time that I had ever stayed away from home.

Whilst there, I learned to play a fascinating new game called 'Monopoly', and Charles said that he would try to obtain the game for me. Unfortunately, because of the war shortages, this game was almost impossible to come by, and I never did get the proper game. However, not to be outdone, I decided to make my own version, and drew it out on the back of a wooden hoop-la board. I made card money, and also wrote out cards for the properties, etc. For houses, I had little pieces of white wood, and for hotels, I used little pieces of red mahogany wood. I had remembered nearly all of the correct names of the properties except for three, so I substituted other names for those three. This game was very popular with my chums, and we would have marathon Monopoly sessions in the loft on wet days.

Chapter Twelve

The War Escalates

Following on from the eight-month 'phoney war', which was the name given to the period of time from September 1939 to the early months of 1940, during which only limited military operations were carried out on the far-off border between France and Germany, the war eventually came to the East Neuk of Fife in the form of occasional raids on the local area by German planes.

Several bombs were dropped onto the fields and countryside at the back of Cellardyke during the summer of 1940 and, for souvenirs, we would hunt around the bomb craters for pieces of shrapnel.

The horror of war was finally brought home to me on the 25th of October 1940, however, when the town of Cellardyke itself was bombed by enemy aircraft.

Along with several other boys of my age, I was playing with 'girds and tyres' in School Road, beside the front playground of Cellardyke School. Suddenly, we heard the engines of an aeroplane, and then some loud bangs, together with the staccato noise of machine gun fire.

Because all of this noise was getting louder, we realised that the plane must be coming our way, so we dived close into the side of the playground wall, to find some shelter. I was frightened to look up, and therefore did not see the German plane going almost over our heads, as it crossed very low over Rodger Street.

There was then an almighty explosion, when a bomb hit the loft and coal-cellar of No. 6, Rodger Street. We were all very terrified, so I ran home as fast as I possibly could. Just as I passed the bottom of Rodger Street, I saw this cloud of pulverised coal dust hanging in the air, just where the bomb had exploded.

When I reached home, I got under the table and sat there shaking, as I thought that more planes might be coming to drop more bombs. After a while, when it became apparent that there were no more planes, I emerged from under the table, to find that all of the rear windows of the house had been blown in.

My grandmother, who was an invalid and confined to her chair, had been sitting by the side of the fire throughout the raid, with my grandfather sitting opposite her; luckily, both of them had been shielded from the blast.

Wardens then came along the street to inform us that there was an unexploded bomb in the garden of No. 10, West Forth Street, only three doors away from our house. We were told that we would all have to move out because of the possibility that this bomb might explode.

My grandmother consequently had to be carried in her padded chair along the street, and our first place of refuge was at Hugh Gourlay's house at No. 22 West Forth Street. We were only there about an hour, when we were told that we were still not far enough away from the bomb. So, we moved again to my Uncle Willie's house at No. 14, Burnside Terrace.

When there, it was noticed that my grandfather looked very pale, and everyone thought that he had been taken ill during the incident. However, when he took his cap off, we discovered what the trouble was. When the Rodger Street bomb had exploded, grey soot had been loosened inside our chimney, then had fallen down and settled in his upturned cap, which had been lying in front of the fire. When he then put it on, some of the grey ash had fallen out, and hid most of the colour in his cheeks, giving him a grey pallor.

We stayed at Uncle Willie's for only one night, as we were then told to move again, because his house was on the route which was to be taken by the bomb disposal squad, when they were removing the unexploded bomb. So, on the Saturday, we moved yet again to my Uncle David's house at No. 31 Rodger Street, and we remained there until it was safe to return home to our own house, on the following Tuesday. Later that day I was taken to see the huge hole from where the unexploded bomb had been removed.

The R.N.A.S. aerodrome, H.M.S. Jackdaw, located about five miles to the east of Cellardyke near the small fishing village of Crail, was a popular place for boys to cycle along to. By going down to Roome Bay, on the eastern side of the village, we could watch the war planes take off and land.

One Saturday morning, I went along to Roome Bay for a cycle run with my chum Wullie Motion, and on the way back we climbed part of the way up a small tower in Temple Crescent, which housed one of the leading lights used to guide boats into Crail harbour.

After a few minutes, we left Temple Crescent and began to head for home, but after we had cycled just over a mile we heard the sound of the air-raid sirens. We stopped to look behind us at the aeroplane activity that was taking place over Crail, and saw some bombs drop away from one enemy plane.

One of these bombs scored a direct hit on a house directly opposite the tower that we had been climbing just twenty minutes earlier. The house was completely demolished and, had we still been on the tower when the bomb was dropped, we would in all probability have been killed by the blast!

Savings schemes, to help pay for the war, were taking place regularly, and special weeks were designated for specific purposes, with activities such as parades, competitions and entertainments arranged to raise money for the war effort.

There was a 'Wings for Victory' week, a 'Salute the Soldier' week and a 'Warship Week'. In the Warship Week, which was held in 1941, a competition was organized to find which boy could make the best model replica of H.M.S. Newcastle, a City class cruiser.

Plans for the model were handed out at school, and my Uncle George said that he would 'help' me make my entry for the competition. I certainly did make some parts for it; including the little deck-houses and gun-turrets, all under his supervision, but George made most of the model.

There were about twelve entries in the competition and, when the panel of judges interviewed all of the contestants, and inspected the entries, it was clear that apart from only one entry, the models had not been made entirely by the boys themselves. I had been truthful with the judges, but some boys still claimed that they alone had made the models, without any adult help.

My model was declared the winner, and I was awarded a fifteen shillings savings certificate as First Prize. The boy who really did make his own model without any help was called Tom Bruce, and he was the son of a farm-worker at Kilrenny Mill farm. His entry was quite an ugly looking boat, and was nowhere near the quality of the other entries, but because it was entirely his own work, and because it had been made in the spirit for which the competition was originally intended, he was given five shillings worth of Savings stamps as Second Prize.

Because of the war, many things did have to change, though quite a lot of the old games were still played just as much as ever. However, the war gave us some new forms of play that we would not have had under other circumstances.

One such game involved the use of large cable drums, which had been used to transport electrical cables across to the Isle of May, where a large gun emplacement was being installed. The drums were subsequently abandoned on the middle pier at Anstruther harbour, and came in various sizes, but most were about four to six feet in diameter, with a centre frame of about two feet in it diameter. We found that, by standing on this centre part, we could propel the drums forwards or backwards by moving our feet accordingly. Some good speeds were obtained up and down the middle pier, and racing competitions were held. I do not know how we managed to prevent it happening, but there were never any instances of anyone falling over the edge of the pier into the harbour.

In July, 1942, my grandmother died, with the crippling disease of Rheumatoid Arthritis having finally taken its toll. As part of the grieving process, my grandfather expressed a desire to go back to visit her birthplace of Eyemouth, on the opposite shore of the Forth estuary; a place he hadn't visited since giving up going to the sea many years previously. As it was still the school summer holidays, I was allowed to accompany him, along with Aunt Phemie, and it was arranged that we would all be accommodated during our stay by my grandfather's nieces.

We made the long journey by train from Anstruther along the south shores of Fife and over the Forth Bridge to Edinburgh, before continuing on to Berwick-on-Tweed, from where we completing the remainder of the journey to Eyemouth by taxi. My grandfather stayed with one niece, Mrs. Nellie Miller, and Phemie and I stayed with another niece, Mrs. Lizzie Cowe, in Albert Road.

Despite the trip being a melancholy one for us all, due to the passing of my grandmother just weeks earlier, these few days spent in Eyemouth were the closest I had ever had to what could be called a holiday. As it was still summertime, the town was busy with holiday-makers, all keen to enjoy the summer sunshine and try as best as they could to forget the war which was now in its third year.

I have one abiding memory of this visit to my grandmother's home town. One of Nellie Miller's sons was home on leave from the R.A.F., and he took me out in a rowing boat, which he had hired at the harbour. We fished with hand-lines, caught a few flounders, and spent an enjoyable afternoon together; the war and life's other heartaches put briefly to the back of our minds.

Chapter Thirteen

A Friendly Invasion

In 1942, the East Neuk of Fife was invaded, not by the Germans, but by friendly invaders in the shape of soldiers of the Polish army. They organised themselves into various small units, which were accommodated in halls and other buildings in several of the villages around the east Fife coast.

Most of these Poles had managed to flee from their native country, and had found their way to Britain by various means, where they eventually enlisted into the new Polish Army, which was being organised by General Władysław Sikorski, the exiled Polish Prime Minister.

The units which came to the East Neuk were brought here to train as paratroops, under Brigadier Sosabowski, who was head of the Polish Parachute Brigade. A unit of about forty of these soldiers, with their junior Non Commissioned Officers (N.C.O.'s), were quartered in Cellardyke Town Hall for a couple of years or so; with the officers and senior N.C.O.'s billeted as lodgers in private houses in Cellardyke.

With other boys of my own age, I was fascinated to see and hear these foreigners forming up in James Street, and marching away daily, to make their way through Anstruther and along the road to the neighbouring town of Pittenweem, on their way to the training ground. This had been set up for them at the top end of the Pittenweem Rovers football ground, near Pittenweem railway station. While there, they practised the basic techniques of parachute jumping from platforms, specially built for that purpose. Later in their training, they jumped from real aircraft along at Kincraig, near Elie.

CellardykeTown Hall, where the Polish soldiers were billeted.

As they marched, they would often sing songs in Polish, and this was a novelty indeed, providing free entertainment for any onlooker. In their billets at Cellardyke Town Hall, their double-tier beds were made from rough off-cuts from trees, which had been obtained from a local saw-mill. Some of the bark was still attached to this wood, and the mattresses were simply large bags filled with straw.

The accommodation and sleeping conditions were very sparse, and the Cellardyke folk tried hard to help the Polish soldiers by making their living quarters a bit more comfortable, and by giving them a gramophone and records. The gramophone and records proved to be very popular, and the soldiers eventually learned to sing some Scottish songs; one of their favourites being 'Loch Lomond'.

We schoolboys were quick to make friends with these soldiers, many of whom had been young students in their own country. One of them was a very good accordionist, and another had us marvelling at his 'sleight of hand' magic tricks, making coins disappear and then finding them again as if they had come out of our ears.

However, to begin with, there was a language problem, as nearly all of the Poles could not speak a word of English, though some were quite fluent in French. Later that year, when many of us boys were in our first year at the WaidAcademy, and taking French as a subject, we seized the opportunity to try out our French on the soldiers, and so a new English/French/Polish dictionary was made up, and entered into a school jotter. From then on, the young Dykers and the Poles were in business, and I still remember a few of these Polish words: "Djin dobre", which means Good Day; "Tac" which means Yes, and "Niet" which means No.

We even taught them some of the local Cellardyke dialect, which sometimes caused the locals to go into fits of laughter when they heard it being used in the local shops. I remember one soldier going into Cellardyke Post Office, and quite seriously asking for a 'tuppence-bawbee' stamp, which gave Fergie Bowman, the Post-Master, a good laugh.

One of the Poles, who had been stationed previously down in Lancashire, and who had a girl-friend there, even asked me to check over his love-letters, in order to make sure that his grammar and spelling were correct. He must have wanted to make a good impression!

When there were any fund-raising parades or concerts in the town, the Poles usually took part. At these parades, they were well-drilled, and looked very smart, with the officers wearing bright red caps which were diamond-shaped on top. When passing the Saluting Dais (a raised platform from where the troops were reviewed), they always marched past using the 'goose-step' as a salute to our town Provost, or whoever was taking the salute.

When their training was finally completed, the soldiers moved down south to Peterborough, to re-group and await their chance to fight the Germans. Many of these Polish paratroops went in with the British paratroops for the ill-fated Arnhem drop, and those who survived then continued with the invasion of Germany. At the end of the war, a few of the Poles came back to the east of Fife, and married girls whom they had met previously when stationed in the East Neuk.

Chapter Fourteen

The WaidAcademy

When the school holidays were over in the summer of 1942, I became a pupil at the Waid Academy in Anstruther. Having done reasonably well during my time at CellardykePrimary School, I was lucky enough to be put into Class 1A, with over 30 other pupils. Since I was only eleven years and four months old, I was the youngest pupil in the school, and managed to hold that claim for a whole year.

Being in the same class as bright pupils from the other local schools, however, I found it more difficult to maintain my previous position as one of the better pupils, and mostly had to make do with being in the middle of the class.

My favourite subjects, Arithmetic, Algebra, Geometry and Science, were the ones I was good at, because they held my interest more than the others. In the class examinations for these subjects I was usually placed amongst the top half dozen pupils. At English, French, Latin, History and Geography, however, I was about average, but for Art, Music and Gymnastics, it has to be said I was rather poor.

In order to enhance my appreciation of music, I had a few lessons learning to play the organ under the supervision of Miss Mitchell in Anstruther, and this considerably improved my musical ability.

Incidentally, it was only after I had left school that I became very interested in History, and I was in the Army before I found out that I was actually a good cross-country runner. This could well have been because, during my school years, I had always used my bicycle to get around, and had never found the need to run anywhere.

Together with many other boys who were now attending the Waid, I became a member of the Murray Library in Anstruther for the annual subscription of two shillings and sixpence. With one of my class-mates, Bill Motion, I would stop at the Library for a quarter of an hour or so on the way back to school after lunch, and have a look at the magazines in the reading room. The favourite ones were the 'National Geographic', the 'Sphere' and 'Wide World'.

The 'Sphere' was extremely popular with boys, as it contained many photographs and drawings about the war. It arrived in the reading room every Saturday morning, and often there were as many as a dozen boys there, sitting and waiting for their turn to get a look at it. The 'Wide World' was also a favourite of mine, as it was full of short adventure stories.

In the early spring of 1943, the herring fishing was in full swing, or as much as it could be with all the war-time restrictions. Early one evening, I was going down the pier when I saw a small group of friends aboard an Arbroath boat, the 'Ben Venuto' which was untying its ropes.

They shouted to me that the crew were allowing them to accompany them on a short trip out to the fishing, and to hurry up and get on board, as they were about to sail. I was a bit hesitant, and so, before I could scramble across the other boats, which were lying between the 'Ben Venuto' and the pier, the boat had moved too far away for me to jump on board.

I tried to get back to dry land, but the other boats, including the one I was on, the 'Jeannie Smith' from Arbroath, had dropped their moorings by this time, and were also moving away from the pier. The crew were all laughing at me being stuck on board, but said that I could stay and go out with them. A trip to the fishing grounds was an exciting adventure for a young laddie, and it was one I enjoyed immensely.

Not long after my trip on the 'Jeannie Smith', I became friendly with a young lad, Simon Clark, from Fisherrow, who was employed on one of the other herring boats. Despite having not yet reached the age of fourteen, Simon worked on his father's forty-five foot long boat, the 'Harvester', registration number LH 56. All of the local boys had a boat which they had individually adopted, and the 'Harvester' became mine. We all bragged to each other that our adopted boat was the best, and I would regularly draw pictures of the 'Harvester', with much detail included, in order to back up my claim.

In April, 1943, I reached my twelfth birthday, and I managed to get myself a part-time job as a paper-boy. I was employed by Miss Edith Burrows, who had a newsagent shop in Shore Street, Anstruther. As the newspapers did not arrive at Anstruther railway station until about 9 a.m., I could not be a paper-boy during the week as that would make me late for school, so I worked only on Saturdays or school holidays.

My round started at East Green in Anstruther, and continued eastwards right along the lower streets to the East End of Cellardyke, before returning via East and West Forth Streets. The papers did not have any addresses written on them, so I had to learn all of the names and addresses of the customers, and also which paper they received.

There were about 180 newspapers of various titles, and usually a few magazines. Being wartime, most of these papers had only about six pages, but nevertheless, the bag was quite heavy at the beginning of each round. When I worked on Saturday only, I was paid two shillings and sixpence (12½p), but when on holiday from school I worked the full six days, and was paid ten shillings (50p) for the whole week. I could never understand the arithmetic in calculating these amounts.

In the early summer of 1943, my friend Jim Watson became the proud owner of a canoe. It had been built for him by

Jimmy Miller, the son of the boat-builder at St.Monans, who had recently become engaged to Jim Watson's eldest sister, Margaret.

My Uncle George was working at Miller's at the time, and had listened to Jimmy boasting of his achievement with building the canoe, so George decided to build a canoe for me as well. Consequently, on three evenings every week for the next few weeks, our loft became a hive of activity as my canoe took shape.

The finished article was ten feet in length, and was constructed by assembling a wooden frame, over which canvas was stretched. The wood used to make the canoe was mostly scrap off-cuts from the St. Monans yard; the main frame being made from mahogany, and the keel from oak. The fastenings were all brass. It had a plywood deck, also covered in canvas. It was very robust in its construction, and a testimony to this fact is that it I still had it fifteen years later, when it looked as good as new.

Two boys could get into it, but the boy in front had to have his legs forward under the foredeck. Its sides were painted blue and the deck and bottom were painted white. It was originally named 'Seamew', but after a few years I changed the name to 'Lion Rampant'.

A lot of my chums also had canoes built for them at that time, and we would spend most of our summer holidays canoeing amongst the skellies (the rocks lying just offshore), and along the coast to the various harbours between Cellardyke and St.Monans. We also set down small lines of about a dozen hooks, and caught flounders. On a few occasions, we would paddle well out into the firth, and I once calculated from landmark bearings I had taken, and by consulting maps, that we had ventured about two miles out from the shore!

Chapter Fifteen

Working on the Farm

Because of the war, there was a call-up of younger men to the armed forces, and this resulted in a scarcity of labour in most occupations, with the farming industry in particular greatly affected by this acute shortage of workers. Young women were recruited into the 'Land Army', to alleviate the situation, and for much of the farming year, they coped very well, despite most of them having had no pre-war experience.

However, a problem arose when it was time to gather in the potato harvest, as many more hands were required to carry out this important task, and the government therefore decided to use child labour for this purpose.

And so it was that the 'Tattie Holidays' came into being.

For three weeks, around the end of October, the schools closed and the children were encouraged to seek work on the farms, in order to help gather in the potatoes. My first year at the 'tatties' was in 1942, when I put my name down for work with farmer Harry Edie at Cornceres farm, about a mile to the east of the village of Kilrenny, on the road to Crail.

At seven o'clock in the morning on the appointed day, I duly turned up at the pick-up point outside Cellardyke school and, along with about eighteen other boys, got on to a horse-drawn hay-cart for the journey to the farm. Our rate of pay was to be six shillings and sixpence per day (equivalent to 32½p in today's money!).

On the field, we were to work in pairs, and each pair was given a measured 'bit', marked off with sticks placed across the potato drills. Along came the digger, pulled by two horses, and the blade went under the drill to loosen the earth, then the flails scattered the loose earth and potatoes over the ground. We then stepped in, and gathered the potatoes into wicker baskets known as sculls. When these were filled, they were laid in a long row clear of the working area.

A harrow, drawn by a single horse, then came round to expose any further potatoes which may have been lying just under the surface. Carts then came along the rows, and the potatoes which had been emptied out of the sculls, along with the potatoes unearthed by the harrow, were gathered up and taken away to the 'tattie pits' to be stored.

We were worked very hard, and soon became tired. It got to the stage when, before we had completed the gathering of one round, the digger would arrive for the next drill, and it had to stop and wait for us, with the horses breathing down our back necks. We were glad when 'piece-time' arrived, so that we could get a rest!

That night, our backs were aching, and we felt worn out. Next morning, the hard work started all over again, with the same problems of being 'hard-cawed'. Eventually, after a hard morning's work, piece-time finally arrived, and we sat amongst the haystacks to have our sandwiches.

It was whilst having our hard-earned rest amongst the haystacks that around a dozen of the boys said that they had had enough, and decided to go on strike. The grieve (overseer), Mr. Archer, came and ordered us back onto the field, but we refused and walked home instead.

We heard that night that another local farmer, Mr. Clement, did not have enough gatherers for one of his farms, which was at Balneil, near Colinsburgh, about six miles west of Cellardyke. We made enquiries, and were told to turn up at the pick-up point at Cellardyke school the next morning, which we did.

Thus started a very happy association with the tattie-picking at Balniel, and I went there for three years in a row. The foreman at Balneil was a man called Eck Henderson, and his wife was also one of the tattie-gatherers.

Mr and Mrs Henderson always had a cheery word and a smile for us laddies, and we enjoyed our time at Balniel Farm immensely.

Whether Mrs. Henderson, being a gatherer, had anything to do with the rate at which the digger came round or not, I do not know, but we always managed to get our bits finished and have a couple of minutes to sit down in each round, before the digger arrived once more. Unlike Cornceres, at Balneil the digger was drawn by a tractor, but horses were used for all the other jobs. Our pay was ten shillings a day, and we even got a half-day on Saturdays. Gathering at Balneil was indeed a great improvement, compared to Cornceres, with the added bonus that there was no work done on a Sunday.

There were four men who were full-time workers on the farm, and they were also a cheery bunch, who engaged in a lot of friendly banter with us laddies. When our stomachs were beginning to rumble, we would ask them; "Is it no' piece-time yet?" to which we would get the stock answer, "No, its still war-time"!

Among these men were two brothers, Sandy and Peter, and although Sandy was heavily built, Peter, the younger of the two, was a bit thin and didn't appear to have much strength. One of the boys, Jim Buchan, decided to play a trick on Peter, who was coming round with the cart to empty the sculls. Jim and another boy carried a huge stone and put it in a scull, then covered it over with potatoes so that the boulder was hidden. Everybody went into fits of laughter when they saw Peter trying to lift the scull. Sandy, on seeing the trick, ran over and chased Jim Buchan the whole length of the field. He caught Jim near a muddy patch, threw him down into the mud, and rubbed his face in it. No more jokes were played on Peter, and from then on, we also kept well out of Sandy's way!

Dinner-time was also a time for play in and around the farm steadings, and we played at 'Hide and Seek' or 'Cowboys and Indians'. We also pretended to be paratroops, when we would climb up quite a height to the top of a big 'strae soo' (stack of straw), so that we could jump off onto a landing ground, piled thick with soft straw.

Beside one of the potato fields, there was a burn running through a small ravine. The sides of the ravine were fairly steep, and there was a broken-down wall between the field and the ravine. We thought that it would be great fun to push the big stones down the steep bank, and see them make a huge splash in the water. But, unknown to us, one of the stones was covering a wasps' bike (nest), and when this stone was moved, the wasps swarmed out, and we were all stung. I was stung just below an eye, and it all swelled up. The farm-workers told us to rub earth on the stings. One of the other laddies, Peter Smith, was stung just below his nose, so he rubbed earth across his upper lip, which made him look as if he had a Hitler moustache.

For our dinner, and for both of the other piece-times, I took a large bottle of Barr's Irn Bru (pronounced "Iron Brew") with me, every day. There was a picture of a strong man on its label, and we all believed that the Irn Bru was making us strong and more able to carry out our strenuous tattie-picking duties.

When it was eventually time to go home at the end of our hard day's work, we were taken back to Cellardyke on the back of a lorry, and I have fond memories of rolling along through the countryside, with all of the tired workers singing their hearts out as they went.

A traditional perk or bonus for the tattie workers was to get a 'bilin' o' tatties' to take home as an 'extra perk' on top of the agreed wage.

This 'bilin' should have been about half a pail of potatoes, perhaps once or twice a week; however, many of the boys were taking home potatoes every day, and these were taken by the sack-full.

As there did not seem to be any objection by the farmers, I also started taking the spuds home daily.

Being wartime, there were plenty Hessian sand-bags to be found, and one of these filled with potatoes to about two-thirds of its capacity, was a sensible and comfortable weight for any boy to carry, remembering that we sometimes had to carry these bags across two fields in order to reach the lorry, and then again from the lorry to our homes.

Some parents, though, must have been very greedy, as some of the boys turned up with large 'net-pokes', normally used for storing herring nets in, and these were being filled almost to the brim. It was laughable to see these boys struggling across the churned up fields, with these sacks so full that their knees buckled with the weight, causing them to fall into the mud.

It was not long before the foreman decided that this practice had got a bit out of hand, and told everybody that if they did not stick to moderate quantities, nobody would be allowed to take away any potatoes at all.

The potatoes which I took home were always the best on the field, and it was a treat to go home at night and have some chips made with them. Over the period of the harvest, quite a large number of top quality potatoes were accumulated, and these were spread across the loft floor to dry. Later, my grandfather would clean off all the earth, and put them into bags for frost-free storage. We usually had enough to last us until the spring, and this was a welcome addition to the meagre food rationing of wartime.

Some mornings we would turn up at the school only to be told that, because of rain, the potato field was too muddy for any lifting to take place, and so we were sent home.

This was one of the occasions when I would take some pals home to the loft for a game of Monopoly, and the game would start at about 7.15 am. Within half an hour, the excitement had mounted, and our voices were consequently getting louder and louder. Neighbours would then come calling to find out what all the row was about at that time of the morning!

We were very happy working for Jim Clement. Years later, when I was on lineman duties with Post Office Telephones, and passing Balneil farm, I would drop into the farm and have a cup of tea with the Hendersons, who were always interested to know how all of their former workers were getting on.

In the last year of my 'Tattie holidays', the autumn of 1945, I did not go to Balneil, but was enticed to go instead with a group of tattie-pickers from school, organised by a teacher, Mr. Gourdie. We gathered potatoes at Gibbleston and Belliston farms, both of which were on the back road between Colinsburgh and Arncroach.

When gathering on these farms was completed, I gathered for a few more days on Jock Pryde's smallholding at East Pitcorthie, around three miles to the north of Cellardyke, on the Leys Road.

On the last day there, a neighbouring smallholder, Mr. Doig, came over and asked Jock if he could suggest a couple of boys to help out at the 'threshing' the next day, as he had booked the threshing-mill. Jock Pryde suggested Davy Moncrieff and myself, and the two of us were picked up by Mr. Doig in his car the next morning.

Being a Saturday, finishing time would normally be at mid-day, but we were forewarned that we would also have to work into the afternoon.

With other farm-workers doing various jobs, we worked as part of an organised team, and our job was to shift the bales of straw after they had been ejected from the machine. Then, by using a pitch-fork, we had to carry and lift the bales up to the men building the 'strae soo'.

The threshing-mill was belt-driven from a large steam traction engine, and the regular beat and hum noises, made by the engine, belt and mill sounded as if we were in a factory. We really enjoyed being part of the team, where everybody had their own specific job to do.

We had brought our usual pieces and a bottle of lemonade with us, but when it came to lunchtime, the farmer said that we were to go with the other dozen or so workers into the farmhouse for our dinner. Taking off our dungarees and muddy boots, we stepped through the door into the large farmhouse kitchen, and saw a sight that both shocked and impressed us.

The table was covered with all sorts of food: cold roast beef, boiled ham, chicken legs and breasts, meat loaves, hard boiled eggs, tomatoes, lettuce, pickled onions and all the various items that go to make up a salad. I had never seen so much food in all of my life, and, as there was still a scarcity of food in the shops due to rationing, I could hardly believe my eyes.

But, before the main course, we were given a big plate of 'kale' (home made Scotch broth), and this was a meal in itself. For the next course, Mrs. Doig and her daughter Jean heaped our plates with the food laid out on the table.

Both Davy and I had been quite hungry when we sat down, but we were so full now with this unaccustomed amount of food, that we were struggling a bit when it came to the dessert!

But what boy, in those days of shortages, could resist having a go at the apple tarts, trifles and cream? In the afternoon, we managed to get the whole threshing job done by about three o'clock. Mr. Doig said that we had worked well, and gave us a full day's pay.

I have said this to many people since, but I will repeat myself by saying it again here, "That was one of the best days of my life!"

Chapter Sixteen

Sea Cadets

I had joined the Boy Scouts in early 1942, and was in the Bulldog patrol, with the Rector's son, Jim Thomson, as Patrol Leader. We met weekly in the Navigation Room at the WaidAcademy, but I stayed for only a few months with the Scouts, as I was tempted away from that organisation to join the Sea Cadets.

Being a member of the Sea Cadets provided me with great enjoyment over the next few years, and I remained a member until long after the war had come to an end. Our unit consisted of about forty boys, and was commanded by Jackie White, the mathematics teacher at the Waid Academy, assisted by Tammy Croll, the gym teacher, and local man Bill Smith. Initially, we held our meetings at the WaidAcademy, but eventually the Cadets managed to procure clubrooms in a former shop in East Green, a convenient location near Anstruther harbour.

We all wore Royal Naval uniforms, and looked rather smart, though there was a tendency to stick our hands into the pockets of our bell-bottomed trousers, and for this we got a ticking-off from the officers.

We were taught marching and general seamanship, including knots, splicing and navigation. The principles of navigation were taught by the Rev. James Paterson, the old minister of West Anstruther Parish Church, who had helped many fishermen to gain their Skipper's Ticket (a qualification required in order to be in charge of a commercial fishing boat).

We learned signalling, in the form of the Morse Code, by using buzzers, and we were also taught how to communicate by Semaphore, using flags.

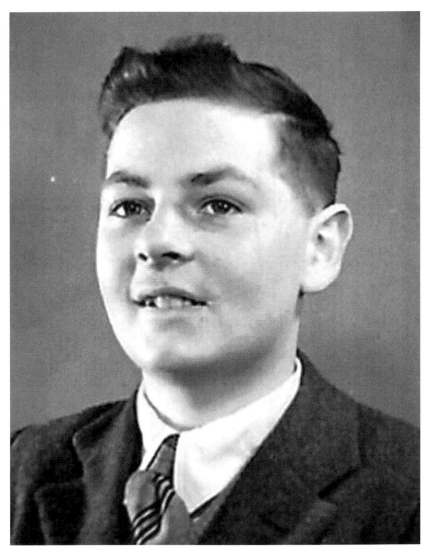

Pictured as a young teenager in the early 1940's

I became quite competent at Semaphore and, together with a boy named Robertson from Crail, was often asked to pass messages at a distance across the WaidAcademy playing fields.

I was also appointed as Bo'sun of the Cadets, and was given a whistle, known as a Bo'sun's Pipe, which I had to learn to play for the necessary duties.

There were five steam drifters and two tugs stationed in Anstruther harbour during the war, all employed on torpedo recovery duties associated with the practice droppings made by the torpedo bombers which were stationed at H.M.S. Jackdaw, the aerodrome situated about a mile to the east of Crail. Initially, the aeroplanes that operated from H.M.S. Jackdaw were Fairey Swordfish, but later these were replaced by Fairey Albacores and Skuas.

In order to carry out the practice torpedo drops, a navy ship would sail down from Rosyth, towing a large floating target, and the planes would 'attack' this target. The practice torpedoes they used were genuine in every sense of the word, except that they had dummy warheads. After the torpedoes had made their run, they floated nose up, and the steam drifters would then recover them.

On two occasions, in different years, the Sea Cadets were taken out for a day trip in these drifters to see the torpedoes being recovered. About three miles off St. Monans, the skipper allowed the drifter's small-boat to be lowered over the side, and the cadets each then had a turn at rowing this boat. On the second trip, when we were about a mile west of the May Island, I witnessed a rare occurrence in the Firth of Forth when a whale was observed about a couple of hundred yards or so from where we lay. We all watched, fascinated, as it expelled water through its blowhole.

In August 1945, together with two other cadets; Bob Sharp from St. Monans, and David Anderson from Thirdpart Farm, near Crail, I went for a week's summer camp with the Sea Cadets to H.M.S. Scotia, the shore base located a couple of miles to the south of Ayr. Incidentally, this camp was later to become better known as Butlin's Holiday Camp, just a year after the war was over.

Whilst at H.M.S. Scotia, we spent our days going out from Ayr harbour in small Navy craft known as 'whalers'. These small sturdy boats, which could be rowed or propelled by sail-power, were so called because they were the same design as the boats that used to be, in years gone by, launched from the whaling ships during the final pursuit of their prey.

My time spent at H.M.S. Scotia was memorable for another reason, however, as it was during that week that an event of international significance occurred on the other side of the world. That event was the dropping of the first atomic bomb on the Japanese city of Hiroshima by the United States Air Force. A few days later, a second bomb was dropped on Nagasaki, and the Second World War was finally brought to an end.

Chapter Seventeen

Boy Messenger

Throughout my years as a pupil at the WaidAcademy, it was my ambition to become an engineer in the Merchant Navy, and several examples had been related to me, from friends and family, of local men who had been successful in that career.

But by now, however, several boys at school who were older than me had written away to the shipping companies, making applications to train as apprentice marine engineers, and had received letters back to say that there were no vacancies at that present time. It seemed that, due to the war, the whole career structure of the Merchant Navy had become disorganised, and would probably remain so for some considerable time.

I had become very fed up with school, and could not see myself remaining a pupil of the WaidAcademy for very much longer. At that time, there was a very limited income coming into the house, and I didn't want to be a financial burden on the family by continuing to go to school and, at the same time, nurturing forlorn hopes of gaining the necessary qualifications for a possible place at university.

The final straw came when one of the teachers started to constantly nag at me for no apparent reason, which made me rather unhappy. Having reached the school leaving age of fourteen earlier that year, I gave the situation considerable thought, and came to the conclusion that it would be better for all concerned if I put my school days behind me in order to earn a wage and supplement the family's meagre income.

There was, of course, the problem of finding a job. For a fourteen-year-old laddie, one of the few options available was to follow local tradition and become a fisherman. Had I suggested this possibility to the family, I knew that an almighty row would erupt that would probably have been heard half-a-mile away; the Corstorphine household being well aware of the dangers and hardships a fisherman's life could bring.

Then, one Sunday at the start of the potato holidays in October 1945, I was sent down to Anstruther Post Office to post a letter and saw a notice in the window above the post-box. A Boy Messenger was required, and any suitable boy, aged fourteen or fifteen, who could ride a bicycle, could apply for the position by contacting Miss Seath, the Postmistress.

I felt that I had found the answer to the problem, and immediately went home and talked it over with everyone. As would be expected, there was a mixed reaction, as a job as a Boy Messenger was not to the high standard that they thought I should have been aiming for. However, since other boys had started their working lives in that same job, and had got on well in the Post Office, I was told that, "If ye stick in, ye'll get a joab ahent the coonter, an' ye'll be a' richt then!".

And so it was that I went to see Miss Seath, the postmistress, and as there were no other applicants, I got the job, and started work on Monday, 24th October, 1945. I was the junior of two Boy Messengers, the older boy being Alex. Jamieson, and the job consisted of sitting around in the boiler-room, keeping it clean and stoking the boiler, and reading comics while waiting for a bell to ring, to let us know that there was a telegram to deliver.

In those days, there were very few people with a telephone in their homes and, in order to keep in touch with friends and relatives, the normal method of communication was by written letter. To get more urgent messages through to people, however, telegrams were sent. These telegrams, often called 'wires' because the messages had to be transmitted over the telegraph wires, were short messages, often originating in distant parts of the country. They were forwarded in stages until, arriving at their destination in Anstruther, they would be reproduced on a teleprinter in the Post Office less than an hour after they had been originated. Impressive at the time, but a far cry from the instant emails and text messages that we are familiar with today.

The telegram service was available from 8am. until 7.30pm., so we had to work in two shifts, which changed over every week. The early shift was from 8am. until 12 noon, then from 1pm. to 4.15pm. The late shift was from 9am. until 1pm., then from 4.15pm. to 7.30pm., so there was only a period of three hours every day when both messengers were on duty. We worked six days a week, Monday to Saturday, with no half-days.

Boy Messengers, known as 'the wire laddies' in the local community, were supplied with a dark blue uniform, consisting of a tunic jacket reaching down to the top of the legs; trousers which had red piping down the outside of the legs; a pill-box shaped hat with a black plastic snout, which also had red piping round its rim; a leather pouch, mounted on a strong leather belt, in which to carry the telegrams; and two metal identification badges, one to be worn on the breast and the other to be worn on the front of the hat.

My starting pay was eighteen shillings and sixpence per week (92½p in today's money), with four pence taken off for insurance, and another four pence taken off for membership of the Union. However, it was customary for people receiving telegrams to give a small tip of maybe three pence or so, and we could therefore expect about an extra five shillings per week from that source.

Delivering a telegram to the wife of a fishing boat skipper, if it contained news of a good herring catch at Yarmouth, usually earned about a one shilling tip, as did delivering the congratulatory telegrams to a wedding reception. I felt quite important arriving at a reception, which was usually held in a church hall or the town hall, and having to walk the whole length of the guests' tables to reach the top table and hand the telegrams to the best man.

I always handed over my full pay to the family purse, and found that the tips provided enough pocket-money, which was sufficient for a few games of snooker or billiards in the games room at the Murray Library in Anstruther, and to take me to the cinema twice a week. It also bought a bag of Caley Cranford sweeties every Saturday night, at Ella Ewen's shop, opposite the Regal Cinema.

In the summer-time, if my pockets were flush, I could not resist the temptation as I passed the door of Tawsie, the ice-cream man, where for sixpence I could sit in his garden, with a view over the sea, and have a dish of ice-cream covered with banana flavouring.

My pockets were certainly flush when, in April 1946, all the Post Office workers got a substantial pay rise, and my pay went up to twenty-six shillings per week, back-dated to the previous November.

With my back money and other savings, I bought a brand new Raleigh bicycle, which was of the latest modern design. It had a 3-speed gear, hub dynamo and mile-o-meter, and I had this bike until well into married life. There were quite a few young people with new bikes around at that time, and it was quite common to meet up with someone and go for a cycle run to one of the nearby villages. Occasionally we would venture further a-field, and a group of half-a-dozen of us once went for a Sunday run to Dunfermline and back, a round trip of over seventy miles! On another occasion, I cycled alone to Burntisland, nearly thirty miles from Cellardyke, to visit my Uncle George, who was now working in the shipyard there.

It was around this time that my fellow messenger, Alex. Jamieson, was upgraded to become a postman, and consequently I became the senior messenger. Alex. was replaced by a boy called George Doig, but not the same George who I had been friendly with during my early days.

George also had a cycle, and together we made the round trip of nearly a hundred miles to Edinburgh and back, and stayed overnight in the capital with one of George's relatives. This journey also necessitated a ferry crossing across the Firth of Forth between North and South Queensferry, with the convenience of the ForthRoadBridge still some twenty years into the future.

For my summer holidays in 1946, I joined the Scottish Youth Hostels Association, and went off on my own on a four-hundred-mile cycle run through Scotland. My route took me via Doune, Callander (where a lot of my pals were camping with the Scouts), Loch Lomond, across the Clyde by the ferry from Helensburgh to Gourock, then down to Troon on the coast of South Ayrshire. From there I then travelled east, across to Peebles in the Scottish Borders, and on to Coldingham, on the south shores of the Forth estuary. I stayed in Coldingham for four nights whilst visiting relatives in Eyemouth, before returning home via Edinburgh. I was away from home for ten nights in all.

At the time I worked as a messenger, there would be about a dozen telegrams to be delivered daily within the town, which presented no problems for us on our delivery cycles. Other duties included having to help the postman, twice a day, to push the barrow, heavily laden with bags of letters and parcels, up to the railway station, in order to catch the train to Edinburgh. Occasionally, however, we had a wire for a farm, which presented us with a more strenuous and tiring delivery; the worst of these being a cycle journey to either Erbitshall or Cairns Close farms, both of which were about four miles away up and over the hill on the road north to St. Andrews.

My job as a messenger meant that I was very much in contact with the postmen, and came to understand the system of sorting and delivering letters. When it came to Christmas, there were huge deliveries of parcels and Christmas cards, and all the postmen had to put in long hours with the extra quantities of mail.

One of the postmen was John Watson, popularly known as 'Jeek', who liked a drink or two. When delivering the Christmas mail, he often became the recipient of more than a few 'Thank You' beverages when delivering his late round, and by the time he had reached our house, well into the evening, he was often the worse for wear, and his bundles of letters were all loose and mixed up. He asked me if I would re-sort his mail for him, and of course, I was then expected to give him a hand, unpaid, for the rest of his round. I delivered most of the round myself, while also having to give Jeek some physical support, and I usually ended up having to take him home to his wife, who then cautioned me that it would be best if I did not mention what had happened to anyone the next day!

The country round, which took the postmen a few miles into the countryside to deliver letters to the farms and cottages situated to the north of Anstruther, eventually became too big, so a part-time postman was recruited to do the Kilrenny part of the round. This job was taken on by Hughie Watson, who wasn't in good health, and he was often off work through illness. On these occasions, the senior messenger was asked to do the Kilrenny, Cornceres and Backfields delivery during the forenoon. I did enjoy this duty, as every day, after making the deliveries in Kilrenny, I had to cycle up via Kilrenny Common and through the Innergellie Woods to reach the Backfields of Cornceres.

Innergellie Woods, at that time, were thick with very tall trees, but there was still a very defined, though winding, path, quite suitable for a bicycle. Although the war was finished, Italian prisoners-of-war were still being used as cheap farm labour, and two or three of these men worked regularly on the fields at the Backfields of Cornceres. They were dressed in their dark brown Italian army uniforms, but each also had to have a large light fawn circle patch on the back of his tunic, in order to make him easily recognisable as a prisoner-of-war. Their uniforms were almost worn out and ragged, and had obviously been mended quite a few times.

When I first came across them, being on my own, I had thoughts about them attacking me, and stealing my Post Office bicycle to make a getaway. However, I soon learned that they were quite harmless, and offered each of them a sweet from a packet which I had just bought in Mrs. Auchinleck's shop in Kilrenny. When I realised how pleased they were to get these sweets, I gestured to them to keep the rest of the packet. Their faces were beaming all over, and although I didn't know a word of Italian, I easily understood that they were most grateful for my kindness. From then on, I looked forward to meeting them on my daily round, and I continued to provide them with sweets.

The winter herring fishing was still on the go in Anstruther at that time, and there were many telegrams to be delivered to fish-buyers, with only the name of the company and no other address on them. These buyers could be anywhere around the harbour, or at the sale ring, or at the railway goods yard, or in the pubs, or at their digs, and it took a bit of effort to track them down. I got to know them quite well, and was on fairly familiar terms with most of them.

On the piers, they had their individual stances, where their empty fish boxes were stored, and they would sometimes be very busy there, with their hammers and nails, repairing broken boxes. If I was passing them on my bicycle, and they didn't hear me coming, I would nip in behind them and tip their caps forward over their eyes before pedalling away fast to make a hurried exit, to the sound of some very strong language being used.

These buyers eventually decided that they would have to sort me out, so the next time they saw me coming along the pier, one of them made the pretence of needing to speak to me about something, while giving the others time to get near. I was then grabbed and held, while one of them got my hat and nailed it to the back of a fish box, situated high up on a load of boxes, filled with herring, and about to be taken away to the railway goods yard.

I was only let go after the lorry had moved off, and I had to chase it all the way to the station before I could retrieve my hat. It was now a bit smelly, so I took it home to get it washed. Miss Seath, the postmistress, asked me where my hat was, so I told her that it had been blown off by the wind, and had got dirty by falling into the gutter, so it needed to be washed. I managed to cover up the nail-hole on the top with some glue and dark blue ink, and nobody ever asked me how the small remaining mark ever got there.

When on the late shift, I had a lot of spare time on my hands during the afternoons, and there were not many boys around of my own age to mix with during these hours. But, one group of boys who were also free at that time of day were the baker's apprentices, who started work at 5.30am. and finished at 2pm. I would meet up with some of them on my free afternoons, and it was these lads that taught me to play Billiards and Snooker at the Murray Library.

Another place where I spent much of my free afternoon time was at Scott's fish yard on the Caddie's Burn. I used to help the fish-workers there, and was completely unpaid for it, but I enjoyed the company, and also got a few hurls in the fish lorry with Davy Scott or his brother-in-law, George Allan.

I was also very interested to watch one of their workers, a semi-retired cooper called Eck Hodge, who was often there repairing barrels, and I marvelled at how he could shape the staves to perfection, and hence make the barrels watertight.

The winter in the early part of 1947 was one of the severest on record, with heavy snowfalls in the east of Fife that blocked most of the roads and isolated many of the villages. The extreme cold persisted for about six weeks, and there was very little melting of the snow during that time, with further falls of snow gradually piling higher and higher along the hedges and verges.

On the road north to St. Andrews, a snow-plough did eventually manage to make a break through, but it was to leave a road cleared only to about a width of seven feet and, being so narrow, only one vehicle at a time could get through the gap between the high banks of snow, which in some places reached as high as nine feet on either side.

Many of the farms were cut off and, as their telephone lines were also out of action, urgent messages to them had to be sent by telegram messenger boys. To reach the farms, we telegram boys had to cycle along the roads as far as we could, then abandon our bikes temporarily before climbing over the banks of snow and into the fields. The snow was thinner in the fields, as it had mostly been blown away in the high winds to lie elsewhere in deep drifts, and this allowed us to complete the journey.

It was a very eerie feeling cycling along these roads that had been cleared by the snow-plough, with the snow towering above me on both sides.

On one occasion, I remember having a telegram for Airdrie Farm, when I had to leave my bike at the bottom of the long farm access road and walk the last half mile over fairly deep snow to reach the farmhouse. When I got to the farmhouse, the farmer's wife insisted that I go into the kitchen for a hot drink, and there I saw a new-born lamb being fed with milk from a child's feeding bottle. The farmer had apparently found the mother in a bad way, because of the cold weather, and had brought the sheep and its lamb into the farmhouse kitchen for warmth.

Much as I liked my job as a Boy Messenger, however, I eventually realised that I could not just sit back and let events take their natural course, but would have to do something about my future career.

After having initially thought that my future career lay behind the counter of the Post Office, bearing in mind my family's advice that this could well be the case if I "stuck in" as a messenger boy, my aspirations had now changed.

I decided that I wanted to become a Postal and Telegraph Officer, so following the advice of Miss Seath, I enrolled for a Correspondence Course in Grammar and Arithmetic with Skelly's College in Glasgow. This course was merely a repetition of what I had already done at school, and so I completed the course satisfactorily.

The important thing, however, was that I had now taken positive steps towards improving my qualifications, thereby increasing the possibility of embarking on a more worthwhile future career.

Chapter Eighteen

Becoming a Telephone Engineer

As mentioned towards the end of the previous chapter, I had latterly started to think that, after all, I might not appreciate being 'stuck' behind the counter of a Post Office, and had started to look at what other career options might be available.

At that time, the telephone exchange in Anstruther, as in most of the other neighbouring villages, was still a manual exchange, and staffed by female telephone operators. It was located upstairs above the Post Office, as was the exchange battery room, and this was where the local telephone engineer, George Dryburgh, was based.

I started to become very interested and observant when George was going about his daily business, and gradually the idea took root in my mind that I might look into the possibility of becoming a telephone engineer, as one or two previous boy messengers had done. I spoke about this to Miss Seath, and she agreed that it would be a worth-while career. My name was therefore forwarded to the Telephone Manager's Office in Edinburgh, and I was eventually asked to go there for an interview, and to take all my academic certificates with me.

I thought that I had not done very well in the interview, but was pleased to get a letter some time afterwards from the Head Postmaster in St. Andrews, stating that Boy Messenger Alexander Corstorphine was to report to Inspector Minto, Post Office Telephones, at Wemyssfield, Kirkcaldy, on Monday, 22nd November, 1947. The staff at Anstruther Post Office presented me with a pigskin wallet containing a ten shilling note as a parting gift.

In Post Office Telephones, we were not called apprentices as such, but were known as Youths-in-Training or 'Y2YC's', as we were on a Youth's Two Year Course. Our training included a five week course in 'General Telephone Engineering' during the first year at Kinellan House, the EngineeringTraining School in Murrayfield Road, Edinburgh.

In the second year, we had another course, the eight-week 'B' course, which was either on 'Internal Engineering' or 'External Engineering', depending on which department we were considered as being most suitable for.

My first actual work experience as a trainee engineer was on Overhead Construction with a gang of four other men, and we were based at a garage in Upper Largo, whilst renewing an overhead route of poles and cables that ran inland for a few miles up the Teasses Road, north of the village. This was a very happy time in my early career, and I thoroughly enjoyed the work.

My first time up a telephone pole was unforgettable. One of the engineers, Tam Cleghorn, who was also the driver of the big overhead lorry, asked me to put on a safety belt, and to practice with it at the bottom of the pole, with my feet solidly on the ground. The idea was that I was to lean back into the belt, as would be the case if I was at the top of the pole, and pretend that I was doing a job using both of my hands. This looked rather stupid to me, but I complied, and I told him that "it wis nae bother". He said that when I had had enough practice, I could climb up the pole and join him.

The top of the pole was only about twenty feet above the ground, but when he got me strapped in up there, it looked a long way down to the bottom, and I was holding on tightly with both hands. He then told me to let go with both my hands, but I would only let go one at a time. He then proceeded to take a hammer and, not very gently, hit any hand that I was seen to be holding on with, so I eventually had to let go with both hands. I eventually gained more confidence in the use of the safety belt, and in later years, if working at the top of a high pole, it presented no problem.

At dinner-time, I had the job of lighting a fire in a safe place at the side of the road, in order to boil a kettle for making tea, and sometimes toasting the 'pieces'. The tea was made in 'drums', known elsewhere as billy-cans, made from old syrup tins, with the rim removed, and a wire handle added. We sometimes set snares in the woods at the side of the road, and kept a look-out for the gamekeeper, before going to see if any rabbits had been caught.

Being the 'youth', I was the 'go and fetcher', and often the item required to complete the job in hand would be in the big van, parked at a distance of several telephone poles away along the route. I would never waste time, and always ran when doing these errands. This very much impressed the foreman, Geordie Cunningham, so he gave a very favourable report about me when speaking to Inspector Minto regarding my progress.

I spent ten months with this overhead gang, apart from when attending the 'A' course in Edinburgh, and my next training was for four months with an Underground Maintenance gang, based in Kirkcaldy, but covering most of the south part of Fife. It was during this period that I had to go into 'digs' with Mrs. Robertson at No. 92 Massereene Road in Kirkcaldy.

The duties with this gang of workmen was to locate and repair faults on underground telephone cables, and although this involved some overhead pole work, it mostly involved the opening up of manholes, and working in the cable chambers below the surfaces of the roads. There was always the possibility of dangerous gas lurking in these chambers, and tests had to be carried out for the various gases, to ensure that everything was safe before going down into a manhole, or when lighting a blowlamp anywhere near.

If heavier than air gas was found to be present, then one of the methods of getting rid of it was to lower a bucket down into the man-hole, scoop it up and lift it out, then pour it away downhill into the gutter, if there was no wind to blow it away. I once had to perform this function outside the playground of a secondary school in Dunfermline, and there were several girls, who were just a year or so younger than myself, looking on. They could not see anything in the bucket, and therefore thought that I must be a bit of a nut case. Most embarrassing!

I did quite well on my first course in Edinburgh. One of the questions in the examination was to write an essay about the process of erecting wooden telephone poles and, as there was no time limit set for the answer, I filled about two full pages of foolscap paper, probably about six times as much as was written by anybody else in the class. This impressed the Course Lecturer, and with the good reports also being put in about me by my Inspectors on both Overhead and Underground, it was decided that I was suitable for 'Internal Duties'.

And so it was that I came back home, to work with George Dryburgh in Anstruther; a stint that was to last for ten months, except for a two-month spell when attending the Internal 'B' Course in Leith. The duties in Anstruther were to maintain the manual switchboard there, and also the Strowger automatic telephone exchanges at Crail, St. Monans and Arncroach, together with the junction network associated with each.

The maintenance of the subscriber's telephones and overhead wires in both Anstruther and Crail exchange areas were also part of this duty, and as Crail Aerodrome was still in operation as a Fleet Air Arm training base, we also had the added responsibility of maintaining the aerodrome's switchboard, extension telephones and teleprinters.

My Internal 'B' Course was held at the small EngineeringTraining School in Coatfield Lane in Leith. This course lasted for two months during the very hot summer of 1949, and just across the lane from the school was a fish shop. In the heat of the day, with the windows of the classroom opened in order for the students to enjoy some 'fresh air', the smell emanating from the fish displayed in the window of the fish shop was almost unbearable.

I did manage to take some time off work for my summer holidays in 1949, however, and I was delighted to be asked by my Uncle David, who was one of the crew of the fishing boat 'Boy Peter II', if I would like to go out on a fishing trip, which was to last for a few days. I jumped at the chance, so David asked the skipper, Peter Murray, if it would be all right for me to come along. Peter said that it would be all right by him, so long as I did not pester him to take me back ashore if I felt sea sick.

We left AnstrutherHarbour on the evening tide, and headed east on a perfectly calm and sunny evening. I was asked if I would like to take a watch at the wheel, and I was given the two hour watch from midnight until 2am. The skipper and the rest of the crew went to sleep in their bunks, with the exception of the skipper's brother, Ian, who was the engineer, and he busied himself down below in the engine-room.

I was given a spare bunk, and was not too long in falling asleep after my watch was over. However, the following morning, when we arrived at the fishing grounds, about seventy miles out into the North Sea, there was a fresh wind, and the sea was now a bit rough, so we were being tossed around quite a bit. When I went up on deck to see the waves, I was met with a morning bright with sunshine, but a bit windy.

I felt fine until I was asked to go below and get my breakfast, and on going down the ladder to the cabin, the smell of diesel fumes from the engine-room hit me, and I had to get back up on deck in a hurry. I was then very sea-sick, and spent most of that morning and afternoon with my head hanging out over the gunwale, near the stern. My sea-sickness caused a bit of amusement to the rest of the crew for a while, but when they saw that I was not getting better quickly, they became a bit more sympathetic. I thought that my whole innards must be trying to come up my throat, and I just wanted to die. I knew that it was no use asking the skipper to take me back to Anstruther.

However, by late afternoon, the sickness had left me, and I found my sea legs. I was then able to work alongside the rest of the crew in gutting, washing and stowing the fish in boxes packed with ice. Our catch was mostly haddock, with also a few boxes of cod and plaice. The weather stayed a bit rough throughout the next two days, but I never felt any more sea-sickness, and I was able to do my share of the work without any further problems.

We got back to Anstruther harbour in the early morning, after spending three nights at sea, and our catch, of over forty boxes of fish, was then hoisted ashore. I felt great, and wanted to tell everybody about my great experience. It was my career as a telephone engineer that was more important to me though, and after my brief spell as a fisherman, I returned to my normal place of work with renewed enthusiasm.

In November 1949, after having completed my two years as a Youth-in-Training, I became a Technician Grade IIA and, as such, my duties were to assist various engineers who had some outstanding work requiring attention. The reason that I was not given a permanent post was that my call-up for National Service was imminent.

Just before Christmas, my call-up papers duly arrived, instructing me to report to the 7th Selection Regiment of the Royal Signals at Baghdad Lines, Catterick Camp, Yorkshire, on 5th January, 1950. On that day, I boarded the 06:50 train from Anstruther station to Edinburgh, then had to wait there for the ten o'clock 'Flying Scotsman' to take me south.

The new recruits pictured at Catterick in January 1950.
'Soldier 22320176 Signalman Corstorphine, A.' is standing in the
second back row, second from the right.

Whilst waiting for this train, I met up with other young telephone engineers, who I had already known previously, and who were also on their way to join up at Catterick. These engineers were Rab Burns from Dundee, Neil Livingstone from Bo'ness and Jimmy Grady from Edinburgh.

Apart from that previously mentioned railway journey to the border town of Berwick-on-Tweed with my Grandfather and Aunt Phemie in 1942, this was the first time that I had ever crossed the border and travelled into England.

After changing trains at Darlington, we duly arrived after dark at Richmond railway station in Yorkshire, and found ourselves amongst several hundred new recruits waiting for transport to Catterick Camp. We were then herded like cattle into army trucks, which were covered with tarpaulins, to take us on the few remaining miles to the camp.

I was now to be known as "22320176 Signalman Corstorphine, A.", and expected to be known as such for the following eighteen months.

However, due circumstances on the other side of the world, this eighteen months was destined to become two years.

Chapter Nineteen

National Service

I have to say that, at first, I did not care for being called up to do my compulsory National Service. Being in the army had taken away a lot of my freedom, and I felt that I could have bettered myself more in my chosen career. However, when thinking back many years later to these early days in the army, I would certainly agree that it did me no harm whatsoever and, in fact, it probably did me a power of good, since I was then able to appreciate that there are times when life is bad as well as times that are good, and I learned how to make the best of whatever situation was destined to come my way.

I was placed in No. 10 Troop of the Basic Training Regiment, which had about forty trainees, with a sergeant and two corporals as instructors. These N.C.O.s (Non-Commissioned Officers) were regular soldiers, and their job was to lick us National Service men into shape. We were billeted in brick-built huts, each consisting of two barrack rooms, with the toilet block placed in between the two rooms. The toilet block comprised of four toilets, two urinals, eight washbasins and four baths. There was always severe congestion in the toilet block in the mornings, with everybody wanting to use the toilets and the washbasins at the same time.

Reveille was sounded each morning at 06:30 and, from then on, we never seemed to have any time during the day that we could call our own. After getting dressed, beds had to be stripped and the bedclothes folded neatly and placed at the top of the bed. All of our spare army kit then had to be laid out across the bed, and made ready for inspection. The webbing had to be scrubbed with 'Blanco', and all the brass buttons and buckles had to be polished until they were gleaming. Our best boots had to be very highly polished, including the soles. All of this kit was prepared in the evening, ready for the inspection the following morning. The barrack room itself had also to be made tidy, and a lot of polishing was necessary on its fittings. We then had to fall in on the road outside the barrack room at 07:30, before being marched off to the mess hall for breakfast.

January 1950 was an extremely cold month and, as the camp lay on the edge of the Yorkshire Moors, there was quite a lot of snow lying around. Nevertheless, we were outside, with freezing temperatures most of the time, when being taught basic marching and saluting skills. Daily gymnastic exercises were also held outside on these cold days, and for that we were dressed only in a vest and shorts.

Although I never saw any physical bullying, our N.C.O.s seemed to have just one aim in life, and that was to break our spirits. Verbal abuse was a constant and common daily occurrence, with the corporals sticking their faces just six inches in front of the face of any trainee soldier, who may have made just a simple mistake, and that person was then shouted at until he was put into a state of nervousness. Some of the recruits did break down, and could hardly hold back their tears, but I always tried to react as if it was all a big joke. However, I would have been in big trouble if even the slightest smile could have been detected across my face!

There were some very bizarre instances of how the N.C.O.s used their authority to make us do tasks that were absolutely stupid and unnecessary. I think that they must have got a great laugh amongst themselves while watching us perform these tasks. As I said earlier, there was quite a lot of snowfall around Catterick during my first month in the army, and we were constantly being told to clear away the snow from the footpaths leading into the huts where we were living. However, in the other areas surrounding the huts, as soon as the snow began to melt, it became very unsightly. The solution to this particular problem, as thought up by the N.C.O.s, was to send us up on to the moors to get fresh snow for the purpose of laying it around the huts, in order to make the scene more presentable. Even when it came to our passing-out parade from the basic training unit, clean snow had to be laid around the raised platform, from which the G.O.C. (General Officer Commanding) was to take the salute.

Each soldier was issued with a .303 Lee Enfield rifle, and this had to be kept lubricated and in tip-top condition. When warmer weather arrived, I enjoyed the few trips that were made to firing butts, up on the moors, and I managed to attain some good scores when shooting at the targets.

After basic training was completed, I was told that I was going to be trained as a Teleprinter Mechanic. Before this training commenced, however, we were all allowed to go home on a two-day pass. Having been away from home for just four weeks, during which time I had more or less been forced to drop my strong east of Fife dialect in order to be understood, it caused quite a lot of amusement when I got back home to Cellardyke, and automatically found myself speaking 'Proper'!

Back at Catterick, the ridiculous tasks set by the N.C.O.s continued. When a morning inspection of the barrack rooms by an officer was due, we were ordered to sweep up all of the small shingle stones on the paths at the entrances to the huts, then lay them out again in 'neat rows'. Another instance related to a big iron tub, full of coal, which was placed at one end of the barrack room. This coal provided the fuel for a large stove which was located in the very centre of the room, but this stove was never lit during the warmer months of the year. So, to make the room more presentable at such a time, we were regularly ordered to 'whitewash' the lumps of coal in the storage tub.

At Catterick in 1950 with my Lee Enfield rifle

However, I found that army discipline on the whole was now much more relaxed than it had been during basic training, and even found that some of the N.C.O.s could be quite friendly. Despite this, almost everybody looked forward to the day when their time in the army would be over and, with this in mind, 'Demob Charts' became the rage.

These charts were large sheets of paper which were annotated with the numbers of the days that were left until the date of discharge was due, and these numbers were duly scored off each morning. Having consulted the demob chart, a common greeting was such as "Only 457 days to go!"

Once a week, a sports afternoon was held, and if the weather was reasonable, the whole squadron of about two hundred soldiers would be sent on a four mile cross-country run over the moors. Though some of the men thought that these runs were a good 'skive' and therefore took it easy, I always tried to do well and generally I would be amongst the first five runners to get back to the billets. Consequently, I took up cross-country running as an enjoyable pastime.

Every Saturday morning, the whole squadron had to line up for inspection on the parade ground. All were dressed in their best uniforms, and every piece of kit was expected to look immaculate. On one occasion, I was wearing new boots, and the dimples in the leather prevented them from taking on a good shine. The Staff Sergeant pointed this out to me, and said that I had better get something done about it before the next week's parade. So, that week-end, I heated the handle of a metal spoon in the barrack-room fire, and melted boot polish into the leather, thereby burnishing the leather toecaps of the boots. The result was that the toecaps shone, and you could see your reflection clearly in them.

When the next Saturday parade took place, the inspection party moved along the lines. The officer, accompanied by the N.C.O.s, stopped in front of me, looked at my boots, then passed on. When the inspection was over, but before the squadron was dismissed, the inspection party returned and took another look at me. The officer nodded to the sergeant, who then told me to report to the Orderly Room immediately after the parade. I then had a sinking feeling, and believed that I must be in big trouble for having 'damaged' my boots by burnishing them. When I got to the Orderly Room, I found another three soldiers from our squadron also waiting there. The sergeant then came out, and said that the four of us had been chosen to form the guard for the General Officer Commanding, at the Garrison Headquarters, on the Friday of the following week. My boots must have made a good impression!

On a couple of evenings during the following week, we had to brush up our drills, especially that of giving a salute when carrying a rifle. Possibly, my drill skills were considered to be not as good as the other three signalmen, because it was decided that I should be the 'Stick Man'. This meant that I had to wear a red sash, diagonally, over one shoulder, and a black patent leather pouch and belt diagonally over the other. I also had to carry a three-foot-long polished baton, with a silver and copper knob on one end, on which was emblazoned the Catterick badge. This stick had to be carried in the left hand, held parallel to the ground, and tucked between my left arm and my body. I was also instructed that the stick should lie along my arm at waist level.

When the big day arrived, we were taken by transport to the Garrison Headquarters, almost a mile away. There, we were told to fall in for inspection by the Garrison Sergeant Major. We had been warned that this man was well known for giving everybody a good bawling, if everything was not in absolutely perfect order. He came out of the office and gave us a very thorough inspection. I was the last in the line, and when he came to me, he said, "Put your stick up into your oxter, laddie!" Immediately, I raised the stick up into my armpit.

At Garrison Headquarters, complete with baton and polished boots!

This surprised him, because any of the English lads would have been at a loss as to know what he meant by 'oxter'. He immediately smiled and said, "And what part of Scotland do you come from?" I answered, "Cellardyke, in the east of Fife, Sir". He replied, "Oh, I come from St. Andrews".

We were then told to dismiss, and the sergeant arranged our duties. My job was to accompany the G.O.C., if required, as a message boy for the rest of the day, but since he was not going anywhere, the only task that I was given was to take some letters to the Post Office. Later, the Garrison Sergeant Major wrote a favourable report regarding our turn-out, and our sergeant said that it must have been my shiny boots and my knowledge of the Scots language that saved the day.

The summer of 1950 was unusually warm and dry in Yorkshire, and in early June the heather on the moors went on fire. Possibly some small deliberately planned burning had got out of control, and the resulting fires on the moors then stretched for miles. The local fire brigades could not handle the situation, and therefore the army was called in to help. Our unit was divided into small groups of about ten soldiers who, armed with beaters, were taken by trucks to where the fires were burning.

To begin with, all of this was considered as fun, but soon we began to hate the smoke and the dust flying up from the ashes. We had gone out at about four in the afternoon, but ended up being out all night. In the early hours of the following morning, a Salvation Army officer arrived and handed out free cups of tea and buns from a small trailer, which was a welcome sight indeed. In later years, whenever I saw a collection being made on behalf of the Salvation Army, I remembered that event.

The fires were expected to burn for a few days, and all leave was to be cancelled. However, appeals were being allowed in certain cases and, since I was due to travel north on the Friday in order to be Best Man at my Uncle David's wedding, I was allowed to go home, so I missed having to spend another night dealing with the fires.

When my teleprinter training course was nearing completion, I was selected to go on a further six week training course to give me instruction in maintaining top secret Cipher Coding machines, which were broadly based on the German Enigma coding machines. Before commencing the course, I had to sign the Official Secrets Act, and this meant that I could never ever discuss afterwards the intricacies of these machines and their operation.

After this training was complete, I never saw any of these machines again, but because of the Official Secrets Act I never dared to mention this training to anyone, including my family and colleagues at work. Nearly fifty years later, whilst watching a documentary on television, I saw these same machines being shown and discussed, so obviously they were no longer being considered as top secret.

In August 1950, Communist North Korea, backed by neighbouring China, decided to invade South Korea. In order to prevent South Korea falling into the hands of the Communists, Britain, together with the United States and others, decided to help the South, and so the Korean War began.

There was quite a hush in the barrack room when we listened to Prime Minister Attlee's speech on the radio to say that war had been declared, and that with immediate effect National Service was being extended from eighteen months to two years.

Some of the soldiers were moved to tears. The Demob Charts were no longer of any use, and most were torn up and thrown into the rubbish bin. I was just about to finish my training at Catterick, and wondered where I might be posted. The three postings before mine all went to Singapore, and from there they would probably be sent to Korea. But, when my posting was announced, I was very much surprised to find that I was being sent with two other mechanics to the War Office Signal Regiment in London. This was in early October 1950.

My new billet was to be at Cambridge Barracks in Woolwich, which were old naval barracks that had been extensively damaged by a German 'flying bomb' in 1944. To get to our place of work in the underground bunker, situated below the War Office in Whitehall, we were issued with season tickets for travel on the Southern Railway between Woolwich Dockyard and Charing Cross railway stations. Being season tickets, these could also be used for leisure activities, and I got to know the central area of London quite well as a result.

After a month or so in London, I applied for and was granted a week's leave, and came home for a brief visit. At church on the Sunday, our local minister, the Rev. J.F.M. Crawford, gave me the addresses of three churches in London, which he thought I might like to attend during my time there, one of these being Crown Court Church of Scotland in Covent Garden.

On the Sunday after returning to Woolwich, I made my way to Covent Garden and the Crown Court Church to attend the Sunday service and, sitting towards the rear of the church, I became aware of someone trying to attract my attention from a pew across the aisle. To my great surprise, the person waving to me was a fellow 'Dyker' called Alex. Wood, who I knew from when he lived in Rodger Street in Cellardyke, just a stone's throw from our house in West Forth Street.

We met up after the service, and he told me that he was now working in a branch of the Midland Bank in London. He also told me about a social club which met every Saturday evening during the winter months in the church hall, and we arranged to meet there on the following weekend.

We met as arranged and had a very enjoyable evening, during which Alex. told me that every Sunday after church he went to visit an 'exiled' Cellardyke couple, Billy and Jessie Thomson, who now stayed in Ilford. Alex. had told them I was in the area, and the Thomsons had asked him to bring me along the next time he visited. And so, after church on the Sunday, we took the tube train out to Ilford, and I was made very welcome. This turned out to be the start of a regular visit to the Thomsons' house every Sunday over the next few months.

Because of the Korean War, there was very heavy signal traffic flying between the War Office and the Far East. The teleprinters were very rarely idle, and hardly had time to cool down between messages. This resulted in a very heavy load on the maintenance engineers, and so a night shift was devised to ease this load. Every third week, I found myself on the night shift, which began at nine in the evening and finished at seven in the morning.

The bunker underneath the War Office was a two storey edifice, which had very low ceilings, just over six feet high. The air was filtered and re-circulated, but the ventilation motors also had to be shut down for filter cleaning and maintenance for a period during the night. Consequently, the air soon became quite stale and, because of this, we were allowed an hour's break at two in the morning to go outside and get some fresh air. During that hour, we would walk up to Trafalgar Square and the Strand, where we could have a coffee or lemonade in one of the Lyon's Corner Houses. I was amazed to see the amount of people who moved about the streets of central London at those hours of the morning.

The Festival of Britain took place in 1951, and a special site was developed on the south bank of the Thames. Whilst journeying to and from the War Office in the train, we passed this site every day, and saw the daily progress being made in building the Festival Hall and the Skylon.

During our time at Woolwich, we still had to perform the occasional guard duty, at the entrance gate to Cambridge Barracks, and occasionally at the motor transport compound adjacent to the Royal Artillery Parade Ground.

On one occasion, whilst guarding the motor transport compound on a wet and miserable night, I was kept dry by standing inside a small sentry box. I made myself as comfortable as possible by bracing myself and leaning back against the rear of the box, while each of my feet were positioned against one of its two inside front corners. I was so tired that, quite unintentionally, I fell asleep, still standing up. I do not know how long I had been asleep, probably just a few minutes, when suddenly I was awakened by the crunch of boots, quite near to me, on the gravel outside. I just managed to get myself back into a sensible composure, before the officer of the guard spoke to me, and asked, quite sympathetically, how I was on this 'dreadful' night. I replied that, because of the shelter of the sentry box, I had managed to stay dry. I often wonder what would have happened if he had caught me fast asleep. I would probably have been put on a charge, with the result of being 'Confined to Barracks' for a week or so!

Because of working at nights, we were supposed to sleep during the day, but this was extremely difficult due to the everyday noise in and around our barrack rooms at Woolwich. We were frequently disturbed by soldiers, who been 'Confined to Barracks' for some small misdemeanour, being marched around the barrack square dressed in 'Full Service Marching Order' uniform by an N.C.O., who stood in the middle of the square, shouting in an extremely loud voice at the troops undergoing punishment.

This lack of sleep coupled with the lack of ventilation whilst working below ground eventually started to tell on our health, so it was eventually decided that we should be sent away for a few weeks to an outstation, and thereby benefit from some sunshine.

I was sent on a temporary posting to a radio transmitting station near Pirbright in Surrey, where I assisted in the construction of large diamond-shaped 'Rombeck' aerials, each of which occupied a substantial area of land and rose to a height of well over sixty feet.

There were about twelve of us employed at this task, and we worked most of the time clad in only shorts. The work was very enjoyable and, in a short period of time, we were back to normal health with deeply tanned skin due to working outside bare-topped in the warm sunshine.

After lunch one day, somebody hit on the idea of playing 'Hide and Seek', and the compound proved just perfect for that sort of game, as there were several bushes that we could conceal ourselves behind. Fortunately, we were well out of sight from anyone passing the compound, as the sight of nineteen-year-olds acting like eight-year-olds would have looked absolutely ridiculous to a passer-by!

It was only intended that I would spend a few weeks at this out-station, but it turned out to be more than two months, and I never went back to the War Office in Whitehall.

Instead, my next posting was to another radio receiving station at Bampton, in Oxfordshire, where I was again employed building aerial masts. This station was situated only about a half-mile from the River Thames, and I often went with another couple of lads, on a nice evening, down to the river, where we caught a few small trout. We took them back to the cook-house, where a friendly cook-sergeant fried them up for us.

During my time at Bampton, I found myself playing cricket against an American team. Cricket is a game which I have never had the slightest interest in, but as it was a case of play cricket or remain in camp to peel potatoes, I decided on the cricket.

This cricket match had been arranged to take place in a nearby village, and the Yanks were quite enthusiastic about the idea of sitting around the village green, whilst sipping pints of beer, as this was something which they could 'tell to the folks back home'.

Anyway, their skills at playing cricket were nearly as bad as mine, so the teams were pretty evenly matched. During the break for tea and sandwiches, one of the Yanks was telling us about how he had been away on an exercise under 'horrendous' conditions. To quote him: "Gee, it was terrible - we had no Coca-Cola for three whole days!"

I saw out the rest of my time in the army at Bampton and, on 3rd January, 1952, I was sent to Blacon Camp in Chester to be de-mobbed.

Part of the National Service commitment was to serve for three further years in the Reserves, and so I was listed as being in the 52nd Air Formation Regiment. This time in the Reserves was supposed to entail an annual two-week camp, but I was only ever called on to do two camps; one at Chester and the other at Butzweilerhof R.A.F. station, near Cologne, in Germany.

Chapter Twenty

Demobbed

After completing my National Service 1952, I returned back home to Cellardyke, where there were now six people living in the family home. These were my Grandfather, Aunt Lizzie, Uncle Tom, Maggie, Aunt Phemie and myself. Sadly, we were soon to lose three of those people, all within a relatively short period of less than three years, as Lizzie died in August 1952; Tom in May 1954; my Grandfather in April 1955.

A few years later, my three married uncles all passed away within a short number of years; Willie in April 1959; George in February 1960 and David in October 1964. That meant that just two sisters, my mother Maggie and my Aunt Phemie, were the only surviving siblings from a family of eight children. Thankfully, both were to survive well into their old age.

Following my release from the army, I found that all of my former pals were now away from home, either doing their stint of National Service, or in the Merchant Navy, and I was therefore a little bit stuck for somebody to chum about with.

However, it was around this time that I became friendly with Jim Gourlay, who was a few years older than myself, and lived just a few doors away from us in West Forth Street. We started to meet up on Saturday nights to go to the pictures, and again on Sunday nights for a walk to the neighbouring village of Pittenwecm for a fish supper.

Jim's father, Hugh Gourlay, was the cox'n (coxswain) of the Anstruther lifeboat and, as Jim was one of the launchers, I decided to offer my services as a launcher. Over the next few years, I turned up regularly to any launches of the lifeboat, both for instances when there were real emergencies as well as for any practices. On several occasions during that time, I was also called on to go out with the lifeboat as a member of the crew.

Early on one particular Sunday morning, several yachts from Granton were caught out in a fierce gale to the east of the MayIsland, at the mouth of the Firth of Forth.

One of the yachts was reported as missing, so the lifeboat was launched to go and look for the stricken vessel. When we arrived at the area where the vessel had last been seen, we could not find any trace of the missing yacht. However, straining my eyes towards the horizon, I thought that I could see a mast about three miles further away to the east. As we were looking directly into the glare of the sunlight, nobody else seemed to be able to pick it out, but I was adamant I had seen the mast, and a few moments later caught another glimpse. I shouted to the cox'n, who then made the decision to re-direct our search to the area in question. Sure enough, as we progressed further east, the yacht came into sight, drifting helplessly in the gale with five yachtsmen on board.

We towed it back to Anstruther harbour, where there was a huge crowd of sightseers on the pier, all waiting to greet us. It was low tide, and initially we could only just get inside the harbour and moor at the outer end of the East Pier. After an hour or so, with the tide rising, the boats were then able to move up beside the West Pier to a more sheltered position.

Whilst tying up to this pier, one of the yacht's crew fell in to the water, and I leaned over the side of the lifeboat and managed to grab him. A news photographer was standing on the pier, and he captured my 'rescue' on his camera. Next day, this picture appeared in several of the national newspapers!

Other lifeboat rescues in which I was involved as a member of the crew included the bringing ashore of an injured seaman from a collier; the rescue of a cabin cruiser which had broken down to the east of the North Carr lightship; and the bringing ashore, in thick fog, of an injured sailor from a Royal Navy destroyer.

Of course, after being de-mobbed from the army, I had to return to my former full-time employment with Post Office Telephones. I was told to return to work assisting maintenance linesman Jimmy Robertson, who was based in the nearby East Neuk village of Elie. Jimmy was responsible for maintaining all the telephone lines and installations over the ten mile stretch of land lying between the Fife coastal villages of Lundin Links and Pittenweem.

During my time working as an assistant linesman, I was given a couple of driving lessons by a Post Office driving instructor in Kirkcaldy, and continued to practice my driving whilst working with Jimmy Robertson. After about three months driving experience, I was given a very simple driving test by the same original instructor; a test so simple that, I am sure, he had my 'pass certificate' already written out before I even got into the test vehicle.

After passing this driving test, I was able to work on my own, and assisted all of the other linemen in the area. At other times, I was attached to the local maintenance engineers who were responsible for maintaining the manual and automatic telephone exchanges in the district. I did not know it at the time, but I was eventually to become an exchange maintenance engineer, destined to see out my working life maintaining all of the telephone exchanges in the East Neuk of Fife; from Crail in the east to Elie in the west, and as far inland as Colinsburgh and Arncroach.

As I was now the proud holder of a full driving licence, it wasn't long before my thoughts turned to the possibility of owning a car, and since returning to work following my absence for national service I had managed to accumulate sufficient savings to fund such a purchase. I was working in the Leven area at the time, and heard of a car that was for sale in the nearby town of Buckhaven. I went to see it, and liked what I saw; a black 1937 Rover 10 H.P., with green leather upholstery. It was always said, at that time, that a Rover was the 'working man's Rolls Royce'.

I made up my mind there and then to buy the car, and proudly drove it back along the coast to Cellardyke. Determined to look after my new vehicle and protect it from the elements and the salty sea-air, I decided to build a wooden garage at the top of our garden, which could be accessed from the neighbouring street.

The wood for the garage was bought from a local saw-mill, and with the assistance of one of my neighbours, Jock Muir, we set about the task of constructing a sturdy garage capable of housing my new pride and joy. We were very proud of the finished article, which remained in use and in very good condition for over fifty years until being replaced by a brick structure in 2004.

The Rover did run quite well, but eventually a leak was discovered in the sliding roof, causing dampness to show during any rainfall. I therefore had to remove the sliding hatch from the car roof and fill the gap with hardboard, which was given several coats of bitumen paint to prevent it from rotting. The floor below the driver's feet also started to decay with rust, so I cut out this small metal section, and replaced it with wooden flooring made from old fish boxes, before covering it with a piece of old carpet.

These repairs served their purpose perfectly well during all the years that I owned the vehicle. In fact, many years later, after getting married and starting a family, the car transported us on the long and tedious round trip from Cellardyke to Bristol to visit my in-laws. The old Rover did us proud, with absolutely no mishaps to report over the course of the near 850-mile round trip. Sadly, not long after the Bristol trip, we decided it was time to part company with the car, as we required money to enable us to purchase our first television.

I had many hobbies and interests during the years following my release from the army and, keen to find an outdoor hobby to make the most of the weather during the summer months, I decided to join the East Fife Model Sailing Club, which met to sail and race model yachts in the Cardinal Steps Bathing Pond, an outdoor salt-water pool at the eastern end of Cellardyke. I purchased a second-hand model of a 'six-metre class' yacht named 'Petunia'from fellow club member David Wood, who had built the yacht himself. A few years later, soon after I had become engaged to my future wife Shirley, I changed the name of this model yacht to 'Shirley Ann'.

I enjoyed the company of those associated with the club and, on several occasions, we travelled to Stobsmuir Pond in Dundee to compete against the Dundee Model Sailing Club. Eventually, I became treasurer of the East Fife club, and helped to organise dances and raffles to augment its funds.

As a follow-on to being a member of the Model Sailing Club, I also became associated with the Cellardyke Improvements Fund, the organisation responsible for running the Cardinal Steps Bathing Pool and the adjacent Putting Green. I was eventually invited to join the committee of this fund, and became involved in managing the annual Sea Queen ceremony.

In order to fund the development and maintenance of these ongoing projects, the committee organised several fund-raising schemes, which including running dances in AnstrutherTown Hall every Saturday night.

The Cellardyke Improvements Fund committee also decided to organize swimming galas during the summer months, both as a means of raising money, and to provide entertainment for the holidaymakers and competitions for them to enter along with the local swimmers.

It was observed, however, that the local swimmers were not doing so well in these competitions, with almost all of the prizes being won by youngsters from the larger towns and cities. Obviously, these children were at an advantage in that they had access to indoor municipal swimming baths, and they had possibly even receiving some coaching.

With this in mind, three of the committee members, including myself, decided to try to improve the situation for the local children, and this resulted in the resurrection of the Cardinal Steps Amateur Swimming Club, a club which had existed before World War Two. Before long, the club boasted over a hundred members, all hailing from the coastal villages lying between Cellardyke and St. Monans.

During the winter months, the club ran monthly film shows, to help with coaching in the various swimming strokes, and monthly trips were also made to the indoor swimming baths at Dundee, Perth or Dunfermline. These outings were very popular, and usually two buses were necessary to transport the large amount of children wishing to take part.

The club existed until being more or less made redundant when the new swimming pool was opened at the local secondary school, WaidAcademy, where the children were taught to swim as part of the curriculum.

As well as having all of the aforementioned interests to occupy my spare time, I also had a keen interest in boats, and developed a hankering to have one of my own from which I could fish for mackerel and codling as well as catch lobsters and crabs using creels (lobster pots).

I started to look for a suitable craft, and eventually I heard about a small boat for sale in the neighbouring fishing village of Pittenweem; a small rowing boat, just 12 feet long, which came complete with a mast and a sail.

I went along to see the boat, liked what I saw, and paid £10 for it. I rowed it round to Anstruther, and kept it there during the summer months for an annual harbour dues payment of two shillings and sixpence (12½p). There were a few similar small boats kept in Anstruther harbour at that time, all driven by outboard engines, so I decided that I would look for a second hand engine of that type.

The 'Dyker Lad' in AnstrutherHarbour around 1954

I eventually saw an advert for the kind of motor I was looking for in the Kincardineshire fishing village of Gourdon, near Montrose. I wrote to the man who was selling it, and an appointment was made for me to inspect the engine. I duly made the long drive north, and found that the outboard was a British Seagull 4 H.P. which, having a short shaft, was just ideal for my new boat.

I fitted a small foredeck onto the boat to use as a platform for when pulling and setting down lobster creels; re-named the boat the 'Dyker Lad', and had it registered as a British Fishing Vessel. The registration number was KY 84, and it must have been one of the smallest boats ever to have been registered.

Because of this registration, I was able to claim back the two shillings and sixpence (12½p) excise duty on every gallon of petrol which I used. This was quite a considerable saving, because at that time a gallon of petrol cost four shillings and sixpence (22½p). My total amount of income from the creels in any one year never exceeded £15, but I was not looking for anything big in the way of a financial reward, as I was only doing it to enjoy the experience.

I eventually sold the 'Dyker Lad' in 1956 to a lighthouse keeper on the May Island, who intended using it for attending to a few creels that he had set down around the island.

Almost as soon as I had disposed of my first boat, however, I develop a hankering for another, and the following year I became the joint-owner, along with two younger Cellardyke lads, of a rowing and sailing boat called the 'Tay'.

This boat had a pointed stern and a centre-board drop keel, as well as a mast and a sail. There had been two previous local owners of this boat, so I knew its capabilities quite well. As well as sailing the 'Tay', we also used the boat to put down a few creels.

However, whilst moored alongside the pier in Cellardyke harbour during a storm, the Tay lost its fenders, and the planking along one side became almost rubbed through. As none of us had the necessary skills for repairing the boat, we had no other option but to give it away to a local man who had the time and resources to carry out the necessary repairs.

It wasn't long after this that some of the local boats started to fish for mackerel during the summer months, as the fish were selling in the local market for £1 per box. On most evenings, there could be as many as thirty small boats seen fishing with mackerel flies about a mile off the coast of Pittenweem, at mackerel grounds known as the 'Fluke Hole'.

On board the 'Tay' with a sizeable lobster

I decided to get in on the act and, together with Alex. Boyter, a local postman, bought an 18-foot long former ship's lifeboat from Leven, around fifteen miles along the coast.

We replaced the existing small inboard engine with a ten horse-power car engine, which had been recovered from a vehicle that was being scrapped, and re-named the boat 'Orion', registration number KY 282.

On one particular evening, we left Cellardyke bound for the mackerel grounds when, about a quarter of a mile out to sea, we noticed that water was gathering on top of the floor boards, and we quickly realised that we were in danger of sinking. There were four of us on board, including works colleague Ian Gerard from Methil and Hans Olaf, a young Faroese boy, both of whom could not swim. So, a quick dash into Anstruther harbour was called for, where we headed straight for, and grounded on, the sandy bottom in the outer harbour close to the middle pier.

On investigating the cause of the leak, we found that a rubber pipe, the purpose of which was to draw the cooling water out of the engine, had come adrift. Therefore, the cooling water was being pumped into the boat, instead of going out via the exhaust pipe!

In regard to the mackerel fishing, everybody thought that they were on to a good thing, and that riches were there, waiting to be gathered in; but, of course, that turned out to be just a wild dream. However, it was still great fun, and we used that boat for fishing for about three summers.

Like all of the boats that I had owned previously, I also used the 'Orion' for creel fishing, and bait for the creels was provided by either using some of the mackerel we had caught, or by going to a local fish filleting shed or fish and chip shop to collect their discarded fish heads and carcasses.

It was whilst returning from a trip to one of the fish filleting sheds one sunny summer afternoon, laden with a bucket full of the aforesaid fish heads, that an event occurred that was to change my life forever.

Chapter Twenty One

Marriage

One day during my summer holidays, early in the August of 1955, I was walking along the pier at Anstruther Harbour, on my way to the 'Dyker Lad', dressed in smelly overalls and rubber boots, and carrying a pail of fish heads for bait, when I happened to meet this nice looking girl, called Shirley Kingscott.

Many years earlier, in 1946, I had been introduced very briefly to Shirley, when she was just nine years old, and I was aged fifteen and working as a Boy Messenger at Anstruther Post Office. The reason I came to know Shirley and her family at that earlier time was because a clerkess at the post office, Joan Watson, had a steady boy friend, Bert Kingscott, who was in the marines and stationed at H.M.S. Jackdaw, the Royal Navy air station at Crail. I became friendly with Bert's sister Doreen, who was the elder sister of Shirley, and Doreen and I were pen-pals for two years or so.

When I met Shirley again, many years later on this beautiful summer day in 1955, she was now seventeen, and she fairly caught my eye. She was licking an ice cream wafer and I commented, "That ice cream looks nice", to which she replied, "You can finish it if you like" So, we started chatting away for a little while, and I told her about a dance that I was helping to organise in Anstruther Town Hall on that very night, and I left her by saying, "I will see you inside".

She turned up at the dance, together with her mother, her brother Bert and her sister-in-law Joan. As I was one of the dance organisers, my duties meant that I only managed to get a couple of dances with Shirley over the course of the evening. However, a couple of hours or so later, her mother said to me that they were about to go home, but as Shirley wished to stay until the end of the dance, it was decided that she could remain, so long as I agreed to see her home safely.

I did see her home, and it was on an evening when the streets were lit by a beautiful full moon. The sea was also completely flat calm, and the moon was reflected perfectly on the surface of the water.

With Shirley at Patchway, Christmas 1955.

Shirley agreed to my suggestion that we should meet up again on the next afternoon, so that we could go for a walk. We met up several more times during that holiday, before it was time for her to go back home to Patchway in Gloucestershire.

In just these few days, when on our walks, we both realised that we enjoyed each other's company, and eventually got around to even discussing what marriage would be like. In a sort of semi-serious jest, I tied a piece of string round her engagement ring finger, and told her that I would buy her a proper engagement ring when the appropriate opportunity arose. We agreed that we would write to each other every day, and that was what we did.

Later on in that year, I received and accepted an invitation to go and stay with her family over the Christmas holiday period in December 1955. After Christmas, Shirley then travelled back up with me to my home in Cellardyke, to stay with my family over the New Year. On the 31st of December, we went off for a day out to Dundee, where I bought a 'three on the twist' engagement ring for her, and we then became officially engaged. During the period of our engagement, we managed to meet with each other for a few days or more, approximately every ten weeks, with either me travelling down to Patchway or Shirley journeying north to Cellardyke.

Our wedding day, 9th March 1957

We were married on 9th March 1957 at St.Chad's Church, Patchway, Gloucestershire, and spent our honeymoon on the island of Jersey. For the first night of our marriage, we stayed at the Dolphin Hotel in Southampton, before flying over to Jersey the next day, where we stayed in the Grand Hotel, St. Helier. Our honeymoon was made all the more enjoyable because the temperature in Jersey (and also throughout the whole of Britain), for that time of year, was unseasonably very warm, and I went about in shirt sleeves most of the time.

When our honeymoon eventually drew to a close, we made our way to the airport and boarded the plane for the flight home. Once settled into our seats, the stewardess approached us and asked Shirley if she had lost anything. We both looked puzzled, and Shirley replied that she didn't think she had. The stewardess then presented us with our Marriage Certificate, which had apparently been dropped in the aircraft on the way out, but we had never realised that it was missing!

And so we embarked on our married life; a marriage that was destined to last for over fifty years.

There are, of course, many further tales to tell from our long and happy married life together, with many happy and enjoyable times experienced with our four sons and their respective families. Perhaps one of our sons, in future years, will take up the story from where I left off.

Epilogue

Immediately after our marriage, Shirley became pregnant with our first baby, and David was born on at CraigtounMaternityHospital, near St. Andrews, in November 1957. On my way to visit the new mum and baby, my car cut out a few miles north of Anstruther, and I was forced to abandon it for the night at the side of the road. Luckily, a passing motorist picked me out in his headlights as I attempted to continue my journey on foot, and offered me a lift. He dropped me at the end of the long driveway leading to the maternity hospital, and I ran the rest of the way, clutching a bunch of flowers, just managing to get inside the hospital door as the visiting hours were coming to an end. Fortunately, the nurses took pity on me and allowed me a short visit with my new son. I have to say that I knew exactly who he was as soon as I set eyes on him.

As luck would have it, when I returned to recover my car with a work colleague the following day, I was surprised to find that it started at the first attempt.

In the late Summer of 1958, the Troy Wood radar station, where I had been based since 1955, was set for closure and, because I now had a wife, a young child and another one on the way, I thought that I should do something about finding a more settled post. So, in October of that year, I decided to apply for a vacant post as a telephone maintenance engineer at Castlebay, on the island of Barra in the Outer Hebrides. I was called for an interview in Glasgow, and although I was considered as being well qualified for the post, I was turned down because I was not a Roman Catholic, and might find it difficult to be accepted by the local community!

It had been my intention to live and work on Barra for just a few years, until my children were of school age, when I would return to work on the mainland. However, owing to the aforementioned circumstance, our plans for moving to the Outer Hebrides were never fulfilled, and I remained in Fife for the rest of my working life, most of which was spent as maintenance engineer for all of the local telephone exchanges in the East Neuk of Fife.

In April 1959, our second son James was born at home in St. Abbs, West Forth Street. James entered the world in what is known as a breach birth, where he arrived feet first. The midwife at his birth was Nurse Connachie, who had, by that time, become the Senior Midwife for Fife, and it was because of her knowledge and skills that James arrived safely, and also with no possible additional complications for Shirley. Incidentally, it is worth noting that I was one of the first babies delivered by Nurse Connachie after she had arrived in our community, and James was one of the last before her retirement.

The autumn of 1959 proved to be a bit of an 'Indian Summer', and we joined in with many people who were going for an early evening swim at Cellardyke bathing pool. On our way to the pool one evening, we noticed that a house was for sale on the Braehead, at its junction with East Forth Street and the Windmill Road. Shirley had sometimes expressed a desire to run a boarding house for summer visitors, and since this house comprised seven rooms, we thought that it would be ideal for this purpose.

An offer was put in for the house and, because the owner was in a hurry to sell, and because there were no other interested parties, our offer was accepted. We moved into the house in early November 1959, re-named it 'Inchmay', and started the process of renovating the interior, so as to serve our purpose.

For a few years, Shirley was kept quite busy during the summer holiday period, providing full board for guests, at a charge of six guineas (equivalent to £6.30 in today's money), per head per week. We found that bookings were very easily obtained for about eight weeks, during the months of July and August, but apart from that relatively short period, there was hardly any interest being shown by anyone looking for holiday accommodation.

Our third son Neil was born at Inchmay in May 1962, and Shirley now had three young children to look after during the day, while I was away at work. With a little hired help, she still continued to operate the boarding house during the short summer holiday period.

We eventually realised, however, that running a boarding house was not the great money-making project which we had hoped it would be, and gave up the idea. The project did have its good points, however, as we became friendly with many returning visitors. We also had some memorable guests, including the Scottish 1960's band 'The Beatstalkers', who lived with us whilst playing gigs in the local area.

In 1966, a government sponsored opportunity presented itself, where older people could be enrolled in Colleges of Education as mature students to train as primary school teachers. Shirley decided to apply for entry into this scheme, and was accepted. Shirley travelled to the Dundee College of Education for three years, where she graduated, with Distinction, as a Primary School Teacher in June 1969. After graduating, she taught at Pittenweem Primary School for twenty-three years.

My interest in boats never waned, and a few years after selling the 'Orion', I purchased the 'Kelpie', KY 272, in 1966. She was a 15-foot long open boat, again driven by a 4 h.p. outboard engine. I used it for codling and mackerel fishing, and also for setting down a few creels. My children and their entourage of chums would accompany me on most fishing trips in the Kelpie, and it was not unusual to sail with as many as ten children on board!

'SunnySeas' pictured off Cellardyke

After the 'Kelpie', I owned a further three boats: a four-berth cabin cruiser called 'Gin Fizz'; a Loftus Bennett two-berth day cabin cruiser which I never got round to giving a name; and finally a 22 ft. Snapdragon yacht that I named 'Sunny Seas'.

Caravanning also became a much-loved pastime after we purchased a caravan in 1972. Along with our youngest son, Calum, we had many happy holidays in that caravan, and it enabled us to travel to many locations all over Scotland. We also took it on several occasions to Northumberland, Yorkshire, the English Lake District, and even twice to London.

With the new found freedom we experienced during our caravan holidays, we discovered a liking for outdoor pastimes, and purchased a 'Mirror' class sailing dinghy to take with us, which enabled us to carry out some sailing and fishing whilst on holiday at a coastal location. Whilst travelling to and from the various caravan sites, the dinghy had to be mounted on to the roof rack of our car!

We also bought bicycles to take on our caravan holidays, and this provided a very enjoyable and leisurely way of touring the neighbouring countryside.Another activity, which was made relatively easy to take part in because of the convenient access from the various caravan site locations, was in hill-walking. We made a point of climbing some of the highest mountains in Scotland, and also several in the English Lake District.

Another hobby I took up later in life was genealogy, which I found to be an extremely rewarding pastime. Through my research I tracked down distant relatives from all over the world, and this resulted in visits to both Australia and the United States to visit my long-lost cousins.

Shirley and I travelled extensively during our retirement, and together we managed to make five visits to the United States, three lengthy visits to Australia and three to Canada. We also embarked on several ocean cruises which allowed us to visit such places as the Caribbean, Alaska, the Baltic, the Norwegian Fjords, Iceland, the Faroe Islands, Spain, Portugal, Morocco, Gibraltar, Germany, Russia, Finland, Sweden and Denmark. River cruises included the Rhine and the Danube. In between cruising, we also found the time to go on several package holidays to all the popular European destinations such as mainland Spain, the Balearics, the Canary Islands, Madeira, Malta, Tunisia, Italy, France, Austria and Switzerland.

These trips abroad were not without incident, and in September 2011, along with our granddaughter Jennifer, we were unfortunately caught up in the terrorist attacks which destroyed the twin towers of the World Trade Center in New York. We had been at the top of the South Tower just five days before it was destroyed!

It was in 1987 that I first conjured up the idea of writing these memoirs. At that time, the plan was simply to describe only my life as a youngster, and illustrate how different things were in those days, when compared with the lives of the youngsters of the present day. But, memories of other events which occurred in my life kept coming into my mind, which I thought were also worthy of a mention.

In writing these memoirs, I have only made brief references with regard to my children, as I believe that they should be left to write about their own experiences. Having said that, I would like to place on record that I am very proud of the achievements that my four sons, their wives, and my grandchildren have managed to attain thus far in their lives.

Our oldest son David trained as a Teacher of Technical Subjects (Woodwork, Metalwork and Engineering Drawing), and taught these subjects at the Waid Academy in Anstruther.

Later, he became Principal Teacher of Pupil Support at that school.

James followed in his father's footsteps and joined British Telecom as an Apprentice Engineer. Like me, he also became a Maintenance Lineman, before being promoted to Exchange Maintenance Engineer in Kirkcaldy Telephone Exchange. Following modernisation of the telephone switching network, James re-trained as a Telecommunications Network Design Planner. He also has a passion for local history, and has published several books related to various subjects of local interest.

Our third son, Neil, joined the RAF and initially trained as an Airframe Technician. Later, he served as an Air Loadmaster on Hercules transport planes and in various types of helicopters; his postings eventually taking him all over the world.

Youngest son Calum became an Apprentice Joiner with Dunsire and Sons, of Colinsburgh. After completing his Apprenticeship, he moved down to England to set up his own Joinery and Shop-fitting business, and has been based in both Shropshire and Bristol. His work often takes him all over the country, and also to various locations in Europe.

Sadly, I lost Shirley on 27th July 2008, when she died of Acute Myeloid Leukaemia, also known as Cancer of the Bone Marrow. This disease was the result of a blood disorder, Polycythaemia, from which she had suffered for over eleven years.

Can anyone ever be 'final', when writing his or her memoirs? In writing this document, my memory has searched back throughout the years of my life, so that I could retrieve what I believe to be some noteworthy experiences.

Inevitably, there will be some additional events, or people, who have played an important part in my life, but have inadvertently been missed out. Without doubt, after finalising my memoirs, these additional events or people will be then be remembered. Please accept my apologies, if this situation should arise.

And here my memoirs end.

Suggested Further Reading

If you enjoyed this book, you might also enjoy the following publication by **Wast-By Books**, *which is available in both paperback and Kindle eBook format from Amazon.co.uk:*

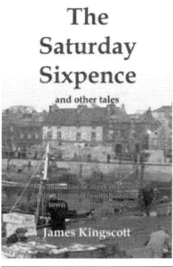

The Saturday Sixpence

a collection of
short stories
set in a fictional
Scottish seaside town
during the 1960's

ISBN: 9798556376090

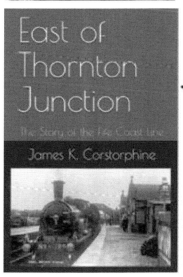

East
of
Thornton Junction

The Story of the

Fife Coast Line

ISBN: 9781976909283

Other Publications available from Wast-By Books:

A Selection of Poems by 'Poetry Peter' Smith, the Fisherman Poet of Cellardyke
(Compiled by James K. Corstorphine, 2000)
ISBN 9798644727827

On That Windswept Plain: The First One Hundred years of East Fife Football Club
(James K. Corstorphine, 2003)
ISBN: 9781976888618

Our Boys and the Wise Men: The Origins of Dundee Football Club
(James K. Corstorphine, 2020)
ISBN: 9798643521549

The Earliest Fife Football Clubs: Fife Football in the Late Nineteenth Century
(James K. Corstorphine, 2018)
ISBN 9781980249580

All of the above titles are available in both Paperback and Kindle eBook formats from: Amazon.co.uk

Just one more thing before you go . . .

Your opinion would be very much appreciated!

I would be most grateful if you could find a few minutes to rate this book on Amazon.

I will take the time to read any comments made, and any suggestions as to how I can improve the publication will be taken on board.

Thank you!

James K. Corstorphine

Printed in Great Britain
by Amazon

13794344R00098